C000075616

HEALII
FAMILY TREE

Dr Kenneth McAll

Originally published in Great Britain in 1982
by Sheldon Press

Second edition published 1984
Third edition published 1986
Reprinted fourteen times

Society for Promoting Christian Knowledge
36 Causton Street
London SW1P 4ST
www.spckpublishing.co.uk

This edition published 2013

Copyright © Kenneth McAll 1982, 1984, 1986, 2013

Kenneth McAll asserted his right under the Copyright, Designs and Patents Act,
1988, to be identified as Author of this work.

All rights reserved. No part of this book may be reproduced or transmitted in any
form or by any means, electronic or mechanical, including photocopying, recording,
or by any information storage and retrieval system, without permission in writing
from the publisher.

SPCK does not necessarily endorse the individual views contained in
its publications.

British Library Cataloguing-in-Publication Data
A catalogue record for this book is available from the British Library

ISBN 978–0–281–06961–3
eBook ISBN 978–0–281–06962–0

Typeset by Graphicraft Limited, Hong Kong
First printed in Great Britain by Ashford Colour Press
Subsequently digitally printed in Great Britain

Contents

Foreword

————•◆•————

I consider it a great honour to be invited to write this Foreword to this new edition of Dr Kenneth McAll's ground-breaking book *Healing the Family Tree*. When it first appeared thirty years ago, it was described by Bishop Morris Maddocks as 'offering a lacuna of healing'. What Morris meant was that Ken was providing a resource for healing the disturbed that had been largely overlooked by the church. Like all pioneers, Ken was much maligned for his teaching and he suffered a great deal of rejection and misunderstanding as a consequence. Yet, around the world today, Generational Healing or Healing the Family Tree is accepted and practised not only in the older, established denominations but also in the new, emerging churches which are largely evangelical and charismatic in ethos.

At the core of Ken's teaching was the belief that some of the personal problems we face today are the inherited legacies of the wounded dead, and the route to healing lay in taking seriously the healing needs of the departed, so that the living can get on with their lives. The second pillar of Ken's teaching stated that the best context for praying for these issues lay in the celebration of the Holy Communion. This was because the Eucharist, among other things, proclaimed the good news that the death of Jesus is more powerful in its effects than the death of anyone else. The death and resurrection of Jesus meant healing, deliverance and release for all.

As you read through this amazing book you will notice certain themes which empower the process of healing family legacies and stories. The first is that at the heart of all healing is the need to surrender and bring all concerns to Jesus. Ken takes this truth an extra mile, underlining that Jesus has access to the departed in a way that we do not and should not. I have always been struck by the words of Matthew where Jesus tells his critics, 'Have you not read what was said to you by God, "I am the God of Abraham, the God of Isaac, and the God of Jacob." He is not the God of the dead, but of the living' (Matt. 22.32). At first glance this statement seems flawed as Abraham, Isaac and Jacob are long dead so how can God be the God of the living in their context? It means that for God, and therefore Jesus, no one is dead and beyond his jurisdiction. This is demonstrated in the stories of Jesus raising people from the dead, an astounding miracle that is often preceded by Jesus addressing the dead, who hear his voice. In other words, Jesus has access to our departed to whom he can address the issues and concerns we bring to him. It is this truth that Ken utilizes in the Generational Eucharist. His book contains a wealth of stories about his patients addressing the departed through Jesus. They apologized to the dead for dismissing them as being of no importance, if they were miscarried or aborted children. Often such episodes included the giving of names to such children in an act of faith and recognition of their equal right to life. Others asked forgiveness of parents or others for damage they had done when they were alive. And there were acts of representational confession for the sins and grievances done by one group of people (related to the confessors) to another. A graphic example of the latter was Ken's description of prayers of apology and repentance offered within the infamous Bermuda Triangle for the sins of white slavers upon black slaves, many of whom were dumped into the ocean as excess baggage to save the slave ship from capsizing in a storm. No further disappearances of shipping or planes have since been reported in the Triangle in over forty years since this act of confession took place.

A second principle that Ken emphasizes is the need to cultivate a listening heart. He was challenged to learn to listen to the voice of God in his early development of faith, and like many of us discovered that he had reversed the prayer of the young Samuel to be 'Listen Lord, your servant is speaking', when in fact the actual words used were 'Speak Lord, your servant is listening' (1 Sam. 3.9). Ken sharpened his use of this listening dynamic, interpreting it as being able to listen to what God is saying about the healing needs of his patients, but more importantly to let God make us aware of the stories which still afflict the departed. These need to be heard and brought to Christ for liberation.

Finally, this listening may also be connected to locations such as houses and wounded places. This is strongly represented in the Bible; consider the words in Genesis which God speaks to Cain, the first murderer: 'Listen! Your brother's blood cries to me from the ground' (Gen. 4.10). God calls us into partnership with him to listen to the lost voices of the wounded dead, in order that their stories and their worth may be recognized and their needs healed. As Christians, we are to be the new acoustic community, which through Christ hears and locates the wounds of the dead in order that they may be recognized, owned, confessed and healed.

It was Ken's lifelong passion that this ministry of Generational Healing of the Family Tree would become a normal part of the church's healing ministry. This has to a large degree been realized, due also to the hard work of the members of the Generational Healing Trust which Ken helped to found. I would like therefore to pay tribute here to a number of those members to whom Ken entrusted his legacy, and who have worked faithfully both alongside Ken and since his death. They are Stephen and Ruth Baker, Revd Peter Hancock and his wife Jean, Lloyd and Margaret Williams and Dr David Wells. They deserve our thanks, as does Ken, and in special memory of him I can think of no better conclusion than the words of Naomi who, when rescued from poverty and distress, said 'The Lord bless him! He has not stopped showing his kindness to the living and the dead' (Ruth 2.20).

The Revd Dr Russ Parker
Director
Acorn Christian Healing Foundation

Acknowledgements

The author would like to record his gratitude to the following people for their help and encouragement in the making of this book: the Right Revd Cuthbert Bardsley, former Bishop of Coventry, Morton Kelsey, Professor of Theology, Notre Dame University, and William Wilson, Professor of Neuro-Psychiatry, Duke University. He would also like to thank Reginald Holme, the Revd Alan Harrison and the Revd John Williams for their writing skills, Matthew and Denis Linn SJ, and M. J. B. Pullen for her invaluable assistance in putting the book together.

1

Awakening

Fresh from the protected world of Edinburgh University's Medical School, I was eager to begin a planned, predictable career bringing health and healing to the physical and spiritual ills of the world. Coming from a family of Congregational missionaries, it seemed quite natural that I should start in China, but it was a country already embroiled in the cruelties of the Sino-Japanese war.

My first 'practice', with some ten million potential patients, ranged over a vast area, much of which was infested by fanatical guerrilla groups. Many times I was arrested on suspicion and held for questioning, once I even stood trial on a spy charge and was condemned to death by a military-style court. A surgeon in a war-torn country is like money in the bank, however, so I was reprieved and allowed to carry on with my work. Four years later, the Second World War broke out and I was trapped.

One evening as the sun was setting I was tramping along a dusty road past the deserted fields in the North China war zone, taking medical supplies to a hospital in an outlying village. This was one of my regular treks, which often involved walking for three days at a time, sleeping rough, being pounced upon by bandits or being taken in for questioning. Suddenly, I was surprised by a man dressed entirely in white, who came up behind me. Pointing to a village away along a track at right angles to the road we were on, he told me that there were many wounded people there needing my help. At first, I thought he was just a misguided farmer returning home late, but his urgency persuaded me to change direction and I went with him to his village. The gates were thrown open and I was pulled inside, but the man was nowhere to be seen. The villagers told me that I had narrowly avoided a Japanese ambush, as the hospital which had been my destination was now overrun. They questioned me closely about my change of direction and knowledge of their wounded and insisted that no one from the village had been outside the walls that day.

I remembered that the white-robed stranger had spoken to me in English and I was certainly the only foreigner within miles. I knew then that it was Jesus who had appeared to me. My mocking tolerance of the implicit belief of the Chinese in ghosts and the spirit world was gone. I understood, too, that the spirit world holds both good and evil influences and I realized that my daily prayer for protection had been dramatically answered. I knew that, however disturbed one's environment might be, a person who had committed his life to Jesus Christ would be safe.

The war meant internment for my wife, also a doctor, and myself – four long years in a Japanese camp, with 1,200 prisoners herded into a factory building, the windows patched with newspaper against the freezing winter. At first, it was each man for himself, jealously guarding his own possessions, fearful of what his neighbour might steal. Then, secretly, a few of us began to meet each morning in a dark cupboard to pray, to seek God's guidance for the camp as a whole and for the special needs of individuals. As more and more people joined our daily meetings, the atmosphere in the camp changed. We all pooled our resources, shared our knowledge, put on plays and concerts, helped each other, and no longer fought over food and clothes. It was the difference between existing and living and, for the first time in my life, the power of prayer to heal in the absence of medicines became a reality.

My wife and I eventually came home to England, weary in mind and body, each of us weighing little more than six stone. Thankfully we settled into a peaceful partnership in an ordinary general practice and for the next seven years tried to pick up the threads of a normal life. But I was troubled. The many inexplicable things I had seen and heard and experienced in China could not be brushed aside. I was particularly troubled by the memory of a 'devil mad' or *feng kuei* man who had been 'cured' of his madness by the intervention of an ordinary woman with a prayer. The man was berserk. In the West it would have been accepted that his 'breakdown' had been occasioned by the intolerable pressures of modern society, but in that remote village on the northern plains of China the people just knew that something evil had taken possession of him and that it had to be cast out by any means.

The herbalist's sedatives and the witch doctor's white magic having failed, the means chosen were as barbaric as the diagnosis – the victim was chained to a wall to be stoned to death. The fact that he did not die quickly was interpreted as an indication that he could be cured, so a special sort of help was called for – not from the mission priest or doctor, but from one of the many untrained Bible women who devoted their lives simply to spreading practical Christianity, but who nevertheless believed in the Chinese superstitions of good and evil spirits. On this occasion, a fearless, pint-sized lady went up to the battered, bleeding creature and began to pray a simple prayer of exorcism in the name of Jesus Christ. The man slumped in his chains, unconscious. The primitive villagers took this as a sign of his release from the 'devil madness' and washed, fed and cared for him until he was fit to take his place among them again. And he really had been cured.

At the time, I was sceptical. I dismissed it all as an outburst of collective violence and asserted smugly that, although I did not understand it, I knew that such practices could never happen in a civilized society. Now, in my safe English village, I realized that mind-sick, 'devil-mad' people could be found anywhere in the world – and that I had to help them, without knowing how. Was it possible that the same sort of exorcism that had restored the senses of the Chinese madman could also work for others? Or, perhaps, it had been simply the power of suggestion that had effected that man's recovery. Again and again I was being faced with the obvious, often disastrous influence of mind and spirit upon the body as I struggled helplessly with the psychosomatic illnesses of my patients.

Finally, I gave in. In 1956 I decided that I must investigate psychiatric diseases and discover for myself whether the accepted methods of treatment were indeed the best way of helping the sufferers. I went back to university, specialized in psychiatry and lived in mental hospitals, learning all I could about the mentally disturbed, sometimes violent people who are condemned to spend their lives in confined places, a race apart, existing without hope. There had to be a way to reach them, to steer them out of their private mazes. I had to find that way. My objective has always been the same: to help people to get in touch with God and learn to live completely under his direction.

2

Breaking the Bonds

When patients come to me, often after enduring years of unsuccessful medical and psychiatric treatment, they can be in a highly unreceptive state of mind, unwilling to co-operate and reluctant to trust yet another doctor. It is essential first to establish their medical history, to check previous diagnoses and confirm that all the obvious necessary medical tests have been carried out: nothing is taken for granted. When a mutual feeling of trust has been established, the patients are usually able to unburden themselves of the 'secrets' that have been the source of their illnesses.

Many emotional problems have their roots in a purely biochemical imbalance which requires medication, and this can be remedied easily enough when once identified, although it is not always easy to discover. But many deep emotional hurts need a different sort of therapy and the supportive love of a Christian community. We cannot ignore any means by which the full healing of an individual can be achieved.

An increasing number of the patients sent to me admitted that they suffered from the presence of 'spirits' or the intrusion of 'voices' from another world which were apparent and audible only to themselves and which psychiatry dismissed as madness. This was reminiscent of the traditional Chinese superstitions about good and evil spirits that I had encountered so many times when I lived in the Far East. Gradually, I realized that the spirits and the voices were real and also that there was a distinction between them. Some seemed to be evil and often came as a result of occult practices, while others seemed to be neutral, harmless voices begging for help. Sometimes the patient could identify the voices as belonging to a recently dead relative but often there was no known connection in the patient's mind.

Who were these unbidden, unquiet spirits? Why and how could they hold living people in bondage? With careful and often painful analysis of the histories of my patients, by listening to them as they began to trust me, and by bringing them to trust God in the firm belief that he would lovingly listen to them and always forgive them, we were able to piece together the answer.

A relationship between two people, begun happily and voluntarily on both sides, may reach a point at which one partner becomes passive and totally dependent upon the other. Frequently the passive partner is unaware of the loss of his own identity and eventually is completely unable to break away from the other's control. This state has been termed the 'possession syndrome'.

Many of the patients referred to me over the past thirty years have suffered from this mental disease, which has meant them living their lives to a greater or lesser extent under the influence of someone else who might be alive or dead, known to the patient or unknown.

In 1960, Dr P. M. Yap, psychiatric specialist to the Hong Kong Government, described the possession syndrome in an article in the *Journal of Mental Science*.[1] His recommended treatment was electroconvulsive therapy (ECT) but he did not record the subsequent progress of these patients. In those days ECT was performed without the benefit of an anaesthetic and the release felt by the patient was probably due not only to the concussion-like amnesia produced by the electrical shock, but also to the extreme stress situation becoming transmarginal, the result being interpreted as a cure. Recently, however, psychiatrists have found it far more beneficial to break the relationship between the controller and the controlled with the latter fully conscious and co-operative. If this break is brought about by transferring control through prayer to God this brings an acceptance of God's controlling power and gift of release.

It is essential to make a differential diagnosis in each case and to classify the possession syndrome into one or more of the defined categories. The bondage of the living to the living is the most obvious to diagnose. The bondage of the living to the dead, whether to ancestors, to those not related, to stillborn, aborted or miscarried babies, or to those who once inhabited a particular place now occupied by the living, can present considerable difficulties in diagnosis. The bondage of the living to occult control is, perhaps, the most dangerous evil to unravel.

Deliverance is no one-step miracle pill to be swallowed on impulse for an instant cure. It is, rather, a long course of treatment, sometimes painful, to be followed conscientiously and trustingly until a cure is effected, although often the final moment of release can happen suddenly and dramatically. First, it is necessary to cut the known bond to the controlling person, alive or dead, then to forgive wholeheartedly, finally, to transfer control to Jesus Christ, making any essential environmental changes to support these steps.

It can be traumatic on both sides to snip the thread which binds a man to his mother's apron strings, particularly when that thread is so strong that it can keep a son from his independent psychological development. Ruth, a widowed mother in her sixties, complained of 'heart trouble' for years. She had consulted many specialists, none of whom had found any actual disease and, therefore, no treatment had been prescribed. To gain relief from her symptoms, she had travelled from hospital to hospital, but to no avail.

I listened to Ruth's tale for several hours on the first day she came to see me and for several more on the second day. She talked incessantly and wildly about her son, never answering any of my questions directly. Finally I became very impatient and said, 'It strikes me that there must be something wrong in your relationship with your son!' The woman became distraught, flew into a violent temper and shouted, 'How disgusting!' She was gone, slamming the door behind her. Soon afterwards she telephoned from a nearby callbox to inform me of the serious complaints she had lodged against me. I felt that I had lost any further chance to help her.

Two days later, Ruth arrived at my front door. I did not immediately recognize her. She was neat and composed, with tidy hair and a calm smile. She asked if she could now tell me the full story which would explain her earlier behaviour. She showed me a letter she had just received from her son, Rufus, about whom she had talked so much. She had failed to mention that he was a schizophrenic, confined in a mental hospital some four hundred and fifty miles away!

She told me that, after storming out of my house on that Thursday morning, and then telephoning me, she had walked about aimlessly for a long time. At the top of a hill, feeling breathless, she had entered a church to rest. As she sat in a pew, she heard a voice saying clearly, 'You have never cut the umbilical cord of your youngest child!'

'I thought it was you, doctor,' she said, 'who had followed me into the church.' Angrily, she had looked around, even under the altar, and found no one. Then she heard the voice again and, this time, she realized it must be God speaking to her. She fell to her knees and answered humbly, 'If this is true, Lord, I will do it now.' A strange feeling swept over her as though she had actually taken a pair of scissors and cut the umbilical cord. She was a changed woman.

The youngest of her five children, Rufus, now aged thirty-five, had been eight years old when his father died suddenly. From that time on, Ruth had ordered his entire life even to deciding his career and his choice of wife. His wife was now in a sanatorium, suffering from tuberculosis.

On the fateful Thursday afternoon, Rufus had felt a sudden surge of release. He wrote immediately to his mother, telling her that he 'felt he was himself again' and that he had asked the hospital for permission to spend the next weekend with his brother. Rufus was wholly cured. His wife, also, had felt unusually well on that same day and, after various tests had proved negative, was discharged from the sanatorium. Shortly afterwards, their baby came home from the foster home where he was being cared for. Twenty years later, Rufus and his wife are still fit and well and Ruth has had no recurrence of her 'heart trouble'.

The controlling bond in a family may skip a generation. Eighteen-year-old Carol was a shop assistant. She began to suffer from strange, unheralded attacks which occurred without any special pattern or rhythm – sometimes several times in a day, sometimes at intervals of a week. During an attack, which might last for up to half-an-hour, she would stand perfectly still in a rigid posture, unresponsive and apparently totally unaware of her surroundings. Psychiatric treatment had failed to produce any improvement or even to lessen the severity of the attacks.

Carol's mother was asked to keep a detailed diary about the girl and from this there emerged one factor common to every attack – immediately beforehand Carol had been in contact with her maternal grandmother, either by telephone, letter or a visit. This forceful lady, who lived some distance away, still treated Carol like a favourite child and the two were constantly in touch.

I asked the grandparents to come and visit me and very reluctantly they agreed. Carol's mother was present but Carol herself was in another room. When I broached the real point of the meeting, the grandmother became very angry and stood up shouting abusively while Carol's mother began screaming hysterically. The grandfather, however, who until then had sat silently began to nod his head and repeat over and over again, 'You are quite right, doctor, I always said it would come to this.'

At this point my wife came into the room, having heard the noise, and I suggested that we should all pray quietly together. I simply asked God to cut the negative bond between Carol and her grandmother. Afterwards, the grandmother said, 'Well, I will have nothing more to do with Carol and I will stop trying to influence her as I am only intruding in her life.' Carol never had another attack. She changed her lifestyle, trained as a nurse and is now a hospital ward sister.

Ruth cut the destructive bond with her son Rufus alone with the Lord; a group of us in prayer did the same for Carol and her grandmother. It is possible, also, to break bonds by proxy prayer without the knowledge of the two who are bonded together.

Two of Miriam's children had died because of her neglect. After this, she seemed unable to break the cycle of ill-luck, or evil, in her life. She claimed to be able to predict the dates of death of members of her family, and this created a great deal of fear. She put curses on several people, some of whom displayed irrational hatred and unreasonable temper, resulting in the disintegration of two families. Her grand-daughter, Mavis, started to have epileptic-like fits which grew more violent just before Miriam died, cursing to the last.

Mavis made considerable efforts to overcome her disability and become a Christian, but this seemed only to aggravate the situation. When someone tried to pray with her, she would curl up into a ball and start to blaspheme, complaining at the same time that she could hear quarrelling voices. Then, unknown to Mavis, a group of people prayed by proxy to break the curse on her and to grant forgiveness to her grandmother, Miriam. The fits ceased, Mavis' life returned to normal and she found she could pray in peace.

Cliff, a schoolmaster in his thirties, was a homosexual. He lived under his mother's protection and feared any relationship not only with women, but also with chaplains and he refused to attend the school morning assemblies. After treatment with various drugs and many sessions with psychiatrists, none of which helped his problem at all, I approached Cliff's mother and asked her for information about her son's early life.

She was a good woman, very active in her church, and had been a nurse before she was married. After much heart-searching, she brought herself to tell me about her own life and her pregnancy. At that time she had been working in a large hospital and was already pregnant. On several occasions, when on night duty, she had allowed sexual intercourse to take place with one of the patients who was an army chaplain. Seemingly, the mother's behaviour had produced some sort of inexplicable reaction in the unborn child which influenced his whole life and thinking in regard to women and chaplains. It is a fact that when the mother made her confession with true repentance, fully shared with the son whom she had damaged so badly before he was born, he forgave her just as Jesus Christ had been waiting to forgive her, and he immediately felt freed. The total forgiveness of the person who was responsible by the one who has been hurt had broken the controlling bond of fear, anger and aversion. Cliff is now happily married and living a very full, normal life.

If the constricting bond is with the dead who are unknown, the first difficulty is to identify the controlling force. The most effective way to do this is to draw up a Family Tree and try to establish whether there have been any excessive behavioural problems or whether there has been any person or an occurrence for which confession should be made to Jesus Christ and forgiveness obtained from him. This is not always easy but with patience and prayer it can be done to a greater or lesser degree of completeness. Since it is being done in the name of Jesus Christ, even the lesser extent will often prove to be enough to furnish sufficient evidence for the identification of the 'controlling spirit'.

There are two main objectives in constructing a Family Tree. Firstly to establish whether any ancestor showed evidence of the same unacceptable behaviour; secondly, to ascertain whose voice, whose unquiet spirit, is speaking to and through the person seeking help – the patient. In the first instance, similar behaviour can express itself in similar feelings, aversions, actions or even certain physical diseases. Or these can manifest themselves in various phobic patterns.

Molly, a well-integrated, healthy, intelligent thirty-year-old woman, developed what she described as 'a new and ridiculous phobia': a paralysing fear of travelling anywhere near water, even for a short distance. Her two children had suffered a ducking the previous summer when they had been tipped in the water from a little boat on a very safe pond. Psychiatric treatment had not alleviated this phobia and she had been referred to me. We did not have to go very far back in her Family Tree to discover that an uncle of hers had been drowned in the *Titanic* disaster. As far as the family knew, no one had committed him to the Lord, so we decided to hold a Eucharist for him. The celebration of the Eucharist where Our Lord is always present is the central act in the process of deliverance and healing. Molly took part and afterwards she felt completely freed from her phobia. Although the drowned uncle only appeared to need a committal service, Molly did accept a greater degree of spiritual discipline in her life from that time onwards.

A very troubled American visitor was referred to me. He knew little about his Family Tree except that he stemmed from the early Calvinistic settlers from England. At the Eucharist which we held for any of his ancestors who needed prayer we became aware of a young girl, sad-faced, who stood with bowed head just in front of the altar. Next to her was an older woman who was being pushed to her knees by a man who stood behind her. The man was tall with a full, dark beard, a cruel expression on his face, and a haughty manner. He wore a dark suit with a large white collar, breeches and white stockings, and a tall black hat which he kept firmly on his head. He did not kneel.

This was in keeping with the harsh and unyielding traditions of the Calvinists, who endeavoured to assert their corporate identity in the New World of America by forcing others to accept and conform to their rigidly held principles and convictions.

My American patient could only watch helplessly as this man forced the sad-looking girl to leave the church, but he saw an angel follow her, presumably to comfort her. It seemed likely that all these years after her death we were the first people to realize that she needed prayer. Because of this, and because of the Calvinist's attitude, we repeated the Eucharist to seek the Lord's forgiveness; then we saw the man kneeling at the altar after removing his hat. And we discovered that there were other individuals in the family who had died in un-Christian circumstances and who were never mentioned in my patient's home. At yet another Eucharist we committed them specifically to the Lord. The vision that we saw then was of the man, dressed in a priest's white gown, holding a crown in both hands. He did not need to approach the altar before the angels guided him away into the bright light. The American, and his ancestors, were at peace.

A victim of ancestral control may feel himself taken over by a force that is indescribable save as a 'foul smell', a 'weight on the back', a 'black cloud', or a 'directing voice'. During such periods, his words are not his own and his actions are not of his own volition.

Margaret was seventy-three years old when her 'attacks' began suddenly. Violent outbursts of temper, unprovoked aggression towards her younger sister with whom she lived, bouts of smashing objects without any conscious intent were quite uncharacteristic of her. Their mother who had died four years previously, aged ninety-six had behaved in a similar way. After each attack Margaret was full of apologies and genuinely remorseful but unable to offer any explanation. When her sister Nellie sought my help we agreed that, on the next distressing occasion, she would command Satan to leave Margaret in the name of Jesus Christ. However, when she tried to do this Margaret slapped her across the face with great force, screaming 'It's great-aunt Agnes! It's great-aunt Agnes!'

The Family Tree of Margaret and Rhonda

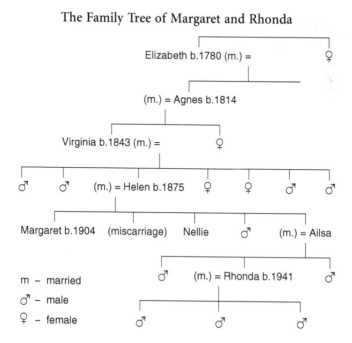

m – married
♂ – male
♀ – female

So we drew up their Family Tree in as much detail as we could and a strange pattern emerged. For the past six generations the eldest female in the family had shown signs of similarly disturbed behaviour. This trait had begun in about 1750 when a murder had been committed in the family. The eldest daughter, Elizabeth, became an alcoholic and destroyed much family property before she drank herself to death at the age of forty. Subsequently, each eldest daughter in the family had had violent temper tantrums at the slightest provocation, down to Margaret, my patient, who was born in 1904.

Margaret's niece, Rhonda, the eldest daughter of her youngest sister, was born in 1941 and was thirty-two years old. She had been having psychiatric treatment for several months before Margaret's case was brought to me. Rhonda had only agreed to this treatment after her husband had returned home one evening to find badly damaged furniture, broken windows and a generally chaotic situation and had threatened to walk out and start divorce proceedings, taking the children with him. She realized that she needed help and agreed to see a psychiatrist. Rhonda and her husband had three children, all male, so perhaps the family inheritance of this disturbed streak in the eldest daughters had been broken anyway for the future.

However, we decided to offer a Eucharist for Rhonda and for the eldest females of the preceding six generations. With two clergymen, one doctor, two nurses, Nellie and myself, we held a service for these family ancestors who apparently had contributed to this chain of violent temper tantrums. Although it was held in private, without the knowledge of my patient Margaret, or her niece Rhonda, neither woman has had any further attacks. Rhonda's behaviour became entirely normal and her husband dropped his threatened divorce suit. Their marriage was able to settle down normally. Margaret once again became a caring elder sister and Nellie's troubles were at an end.

The cutting of the bond, and the transfer of control to Jesus Christ, can be simultaneous and can happen to non-Christians as well as Christians. Esther was a seventy-year-old widow, whose schizophrenic son Samuel was in a hospital on the other side of the world; she was very concerned for his welfare and his future. From his symptoms which were confusing and incomplete it soon became obvious that his disease was not due to a medical abnormality but was caused largely by his mother's lifelong influence over him. I suggested that we should present the problem to Jesus Christ in prayer and that Esther should allow him to take control both of her son and of herself. As she was Jewish, this was not an easy concept for her and she needed time to think about it. She was, in fact, being asked to renounce her faith and become a Christian. She left me and went out into the night, greatly distressed. Suddenly, in the darkness, she saw before her a large, glowing crucifix. This could have been the result of her own imagination as she turned over in her mind what we had been discussing. But she could not have imagined the voice of Jesus Christ which she heard. He told her clearly that she must release her son Samuel to him and also give herself to him. She was compelled to accept Jesus into her heart at that moment and she then felt able to release her son to him. On the other side of the world, Samuel, without any knowledge of his mother's conversion, began his steady recovery from the schizoid state. The mother now calls herself a fulfilled Jew.

A case of repeated behaviour pattern was brought to me by the clergyman father of a woman called Norma. Norma had developed an urge to gouge out the eyes of her own children – a trait more in keeping with sixteenth-century practices than with modern behaviour. We talked about his ancestors and when we drew up the Family Tree we discovered that generations ago the family residence had been a castle, complete with moat and dungeons. The clergyman's family had never been there. We went on a tour of the castle and found a torture chamber in the dungeon containing, among other evil things, implements which would have been used for the deed that was obsessing Norma.

I suggested that her father, being a clergyman, should consult his bishop and they decided to celebrate a Eucharist for the dead in five days' time. To our amazement, he heard that his daughter was completely freed from her obsession on the day this decision had been made. She had had no knowledge of their intention; the hospital where she was kept in a padded cell was more than a hundred miles away, and we certainly would have been unable to elicit her consent. Later we discovered that an aunt in another mental hospital, who was quite unknown to me, was healed at about the same time. The decision to hold a Eucharist had had an effect far beyond anything we had hoped would happen. We still held a Eucharist five days later, but it now was a service of thanksgiving.

Similar physical pathology or symptoms of disease can point an identifying finger at the ancestor needing a Eucharist. A professional man of sixty-five developed periodic bouts of breathlessness for which doctors could find no medical cause. It transpired that his father had been drowned many years earlier when he had been drunk and was buried anonymously without a loving committal by the family or anyone else. My explanation that the breathlessness was an acting out of his father's unmourned death infuriated the man. Three months later, however, with his bouts becoming progressively worse, he agreed to attend a committal service for his father. We held a service and he was cured.

A young schoolmaster came to see me one day in great distress for he had been having a recurring nightmare. Each time, he was standing on the brink of a 'black abyss which seemed to be eternity' and he could not move. The nightmares had begun when, in an attempt to overcome an alcohol problem, he had thought about his religion seriously instead of letting it ride automatically. Eventually, it emerged that, when he was only two years old, his father had died on the deck of a submarine as it was sunk during the war. As my patient was a Roman Catholic, I suggested that he should ask his priest to say a requiem mass (Eucharist of the Resurrection) for his father, who obviously had not been properly committed. The man agreed and the 'black abyss of eternity' never recurred.

When the voices that my patients hear do not respond to conventional medication, I take them very seriously.

Gil did well at school and was a good athlete. At the age of fourteen, on the day of his father's death, he shut himself in his room and wept. He remained so grief-stricken and became so withdrawn and uncommunicative that eventually he was hospitalized as an atypical schizophrenic, spending much of his time imitating his father's voice and mannerisms and conversing with him.

When Gil had been in hospital for twelve years with no improvement, his mother appealed to us for help. Not wishing to interfere with his treatment, I did not see Gil himself. His mother told me that the family, including Gil's father before he died, held no religious beliefs and she did not remember much about the burial service. She commented, 'He was a terrible man. Thank goodness we got rid of him! It was all so sudden and horrible that I just wanted to get it over as quickly as possible. I think it was a cremation, but it was all over in a few minutes and I have no idea what was said.'

She agreed to attend a new service of committal for her late husband and one Saturday afternoon, with an Anglican priest and a Methodist minister, we held a simple chapel service without any dramatic happening. On the next day, a Sunday, Gil was allowed home for lunch with his family. His elder brother and sister noticed a change in him, but he insisted on waiting for his mother's return to the house before he would explain.

Apparently, on the previous afternoon, he was in the hospital library as usual, crying and calling for his father. Suddenly, it struck him that it was selfish to demand his dead father's impossible return to life – a thought that had never occurred to him before. Then, despite not believing in God, he found himself praying that God would look after his father.

Gil added with a smile, 'Since that moment I have been feeling fine.' We worked out that this event had taken place at about the same time as we were holding the service for his father. Gil has remained well and normal and he has never 'talked' with his father again.

When the bond has been cut, no matter with whom it was formed or however long-standing it was, the possession-void must be transferred to Jesus Christ to allow him to take complete control. The patient is often fully aware of this and the transfer will be straightforward. To Christ has been given the care of the controlling spirit and to him must be given the total care of the life that is no longer being controlled. The bond may be so strong that it continues beyond death, especially when it is a loving one. It is not unusual for a husband or wife to grieve for a dead partner to such an extent that they themselves die prematurely, almost as if they had willed it. Widows, in the first year of widowhood, suffer ten times the normal rate of serious illness and death. There is no evil intention involved in this, but such grief could be borne more easily through Jesus Christ.

Bonds between unrelated people may also carry on through death. Where the relationship has been an intimate one, the continued domination by the dead partner may be sought actively by the one left alive. Such a bond must be cut; it is totally destructive. Georgina was twenty-three years old when she was brought to me. She had been trained as a school teacher but had been certified several times. She was known medically as a schizophrenic but many psychiatric labels had been attached to her. Therapeutic drugs, electroconvulsive therapy and sixteen psychiatrists had failed to cure her permanently. Georgina told me that the real trouble was her 'blackouts'. They came without warning and lasted between three and fourteen days. During these periods she would behave in a bizarre way and not remember anything about them afterwards. On one occasion when she was entrusted with school money to take to the bank, she found herself in the street, loaded with useless presents which she had no recollection of buying.

As she was leaving at the end of our first interview she suddenly said, 'For some reason, I cannot lie to you'. She then told me that for years she had had a lesbian relationship with a nurse who had died. For days or weeks at a time she would daydream herself into contact with her dead friend and they would hold conversations. During such times she would lie on her bed completely oblivious to all that went on around her. Georgina and I went to a priest who, kneeling at the altar, very simply cut the bond by commanding the possessing spirit to go 'In the name of Jesus Christ to her appointed place'.

At that moment, the girl let out a scream and then all was peaceful. She said afterwards that she felt as though there was a hole in her head that now felt clean. Her strange 'blackouts' ceased and she was encouraged to adopt a new spiritual discipline. She is now happily married and reports that her experiences have been of help to other people in similar circumstances.

The majority of cases of controlling bondage to the living or to the dead are not so dramatic and mysterious as Georgina's but are more like the often found bondage of a woman to an idealized father, sought in a husband; or of a man to his mother's apron strings.

Harry married the young receptionist in his mother's hotel and the newly-weds continued to live in the hotel. His wife developed a severe depression which prevented her from sleeping. Finally, through a Eucharist, the bond between Harry and his mother was cut and she agreed to Harry and his wife moving out of the hotel to live in a cottage some distance away. As Harry was freed from his mother's control, he began to relate anew to his wife; she, in turn, was freed from her depressive illness. All three formed a new, unbreakable spiritual bond.

The Eucharist is conducted in a quiet, prayerful way. Healing comes to the patient through a peaceful commitment to Jesus Christ as his loving release is accepted. Release may occur immediately after the announcement of an intention to bring the case to God. At other times the cure takes place while the service is in progress, albeit at a distance. Sometimes the healing process begins then and is finally effective months after the service.

In all cases of bondage the best efforts of psychiatry should be utilized to integrate the personality but it is essential that they are used in conjunction with prayer and the Eucharist service which has the power both to break the destructive bondage and to form life-giving bonds with Jesus Christ.[2]

3

Christ's Healing

In preparation for a Eucharist of deliverance, we draw up the Family Tree and identify those for whom we shall pray. In the case of babies who were stillborn, miscarried or aborted it is helpful to call them by name (Isa. 49.1). If the baby had no name, sometimes the Lord will now suggest one or the family may now choose one, so that the prayer becomes more specific and personal.

Next we decide whom we wish to be present. Sometimes there are only a few people at the service. Often it is celebrated without the presence of those for whom the Eucharist is offered or, indeed, without their consent or knowledge of what is being done on their behalf. Frequently, their mental state, geographical distance or uninterest in the Eucharist prevents their participation. But, whenever possible, we try to have the living persons who need prayer actually with us so that they can ask for guidance and, most importantly, learn how to continue to pray on their own at future Eucharists. It seems to help if they are present and can accept Jesus Christ's love both for themselves and for their ancestors. We also invite other loving members of the family or friends who may wish to pray, including non-Christians whose minds are open to experiencing the power of Jesus. The more love is present, the nearer we come to Jesus and the more healing happens.

Usually, we begin with an informal prayer said aloud, asking the Father to gather the dead for whom we are praying, asking for whatever healing we trust will happen during the service; asking that both the dead and their living descendants should receive forgiveness and fullness of life; asking that Satan leave, and asking that the Holy Spirit should compensate for whatever shortcomings there may be in our prayers. Thus we have prepared ourselves for the Eucharist and we are ready for the Lord's Prayer.

I am not a theologian. I am a simple searcher with a limited understanding of the working of God's healing power. From careful watching and listening, it seems to me that there are four distinct stages or movements in the manifestation of that healing power which correspond to different prayers that we offer.

(i) The first stage

By our prayer 'Deliver us from evil', from the Lord's Prayer with which we begin the service, we are asking God to free both the living and the dead from any bondage to the evil one. This prayer for deliverance asks that we may be protected from him and in Jesus Christ's name commands that he be bound and handed over peacefully to Jesus Christ. We are asking in fact that, through his blood represented by the communion wine, Jesus Christ should cleanse the blood lines of the living and the dead of all that blocks healthy life, especially by breaking any hereditary seals and curses and by casting out any evil spirits. In this we are obeying the Lord's injunction not only to heal but also to cast out the evil one (Mark 16.17–18).

Since Satan can express himself both by tormenting our dead relatives and also through human violence and crime, as well as in emotional and physical disorders, removal both of ourselves and the dead from all his invisible channels of evil through the Eucharist is essential. 'You cannot drink the cup of the Lord and the cup of the demons too; you cannot have a part in both the Lord's table and the table of demons' (1 Cor. 10.21). Through taking the Lord's cup we break old covenants with the evil one and enter into the New Covenant with God.

(ii) Stage two

The second healing stage concerns vital forgiveness. By the prayers for forgiveness, the Collect and the Scripture readings we offer the Lord's love and forgiveness to both the living and the dead for any inroads which Satan has made. The dead must be forgiven if we are to help them at the Eucharist. If a patient cannot actually forgive a dead relative he should ask himself whether he really *wants* to forgive, even if he cannot yet feel the forgiveness in his own heart. Unless he sincerely *wants* to begin forgiving and loving, he should leave the Eucharist, for both love and prayer must be sincere in order to be effective (Matt. 5.23–24).

I have usually found that, when the Eucharist does not work as expected, the person concerned is not sincere in forgiving or in loving. The depth of forgiveness must be as great as was the Lord's in dying for that person. 'This is my blood of the covenant, which is poured out for many for the forgiveness of sins' (Matt. 26.28).

Saying 'I forgive you' to the dead can be nothing but empty words masking real unwillingness to forgive, or at least falling far short of Jesus Christ's total forgiveness. In the parable of the prodigal son, Jesus demonstrates complete forgiveness – firstly, like the Father continually looking for the return of his son, we must let ourselves feel all the painful destruction we want to forgive rather than swallow it in denial. If we do not face it, we cannot choose to forgive it.

Secondly, we need to love the one who has dealt us the destruction, as St Augustine says, 'hate the sin but love the sinner'. Once we face the full destruction, we must decide what we want – and whether we choose to forgive unconditionally even if the other person never responds or changes. *Fore-give*-ness is love *given before* another has either given it, earned it, accepted it, or even understood it. It is the Father running out to embrace his prodigal son even before he knows whether the son has come repenting of all the destruction he has caused, or whether he might be returning just to ask for more money. He loves his son not because the son has earned it or can understand it but simply because he needs his Father's love and cannot grow without it.

Jesus Christ allows us to choose between being the elder brother focusing on his own pain or being the father focusing on the son's pain and holding out welcoming arms of healing. The latter concentrates not on the destruction but on the growth which can bring the son and the father closer to each other and to God.

The rite of the Eucharist involves double forgiveness; through Jesus Christ we not only forgive the dead but we ask them to forgive us. How do we, the living, need forgiveness? To identify the often unrealized evil within ourselves and thus be able to confess it and be forgiven by the Lord, we should ask whether we have failed to live a balanced life and whether we are blaming controlling forces outside ourselves for behaviour that *we* could have changed. We should question, also, whether we believe more in the power of the evil one to control us than in God's power to bring freedom. What pushes God out of a person's life? It may be drug abuse, obsession with money or sex, or occult practices. It is easy to compromise ourselves by refusing to allow the Lord's power to enter every part of our lives so that our will is totally turned over to him. We must ask ourselves, too, whether some part of us has not wanted a dead child of ours or has rejected anyone in our family tree; or whether we really forgave a dead relative for something he had done to us or to a loved one. It is meaningless to say, 'I could forgive him anything but that ...' or, 'If only he had not done that, I would forgive him ...'

Sometimes we know how the dead were unloving and in need of God's forgiveness, because many sinful habits are passed on from generation to generation (as we have seen in Chapter 2). Therefore we might pray that, through our Lord, all those ancestors involved in the handing down of temper tantrums, for example, might receive our forgiveness. We can ask the Lord to help them to accept his forgiveness of this evil (temper tantrums) and also of the other evil that only he knows (2 Cor. 5.18–20).

Tom came to the Eucharist with a secret. Throughout his life it had been a source of great shame to him that he was illegitimate and had been adopted a few days after his birth. Consequently, he knew nothing about his Family Tree and didn't know how to pray. Rather than reveal his difficulty at our service, he merely asked to pray for 'mother' and 'father'.

During the rite of forgiveness, Tom could see his adoptive parents on the left-hand side of the altar, and on the right-hand side he could make out a small wooden shed in which were two obviously very poor people, presumably his real parents. Knowing that the Lord was present too, Tom asked simply, 'What am I supposed to do about this?' In answer, Tom saw Mary, the mother of Jesus Christ, who seemed to be welcoming children around the altar, come over to him. This surprised him since his religious tradition did not involve much devotion to Mary. She told him not to worry as she knew what to do and she returned to the altar. There, she brought together the two sets of parents and they embraced gently before angels took them all slowly up into a bright light.

Although we cannot be sure what they experienced, perhaps the true parents of Tom felt as secretive as he had and needed the love and reassurance of the adoptive parents before they could be at peace. As he watched, Tom felt the confusion drain from his body and gratitude fill his heart for all of these four people who had been largely responsible for bringing him to this moment in his life. He had needed to become reconciled with the parents who had branded him as illegitimate. He now felt so free that, not only did he tell his wife and child the whole story, but shared his secret with his church fellowship. Many of them were so moved that they went the next evening to celebrate the Eucharist, taking with them their Family Trees, and they were healed of numerous ills. 'With what forgiveness we forgive, so we are forgiven.'

(iii) The third stage

The third healing stage is perhaps the most difficult, for in it Jesus Christ invites us to bear witness to his death and resurrection as he draws the dead to himself. 'Whenever you eat this bread and drink this cup, you proclaim the Lord's death until he comes' (1 Cor. 11.26). During this part of the service, the people concerned may place their Family Tree on the altar together with the gifts of bread and wine which are then offered to God and consecrated. We pray that even as Jesus Christ blesses the bread and the wine and his life comes into them, so it will come also into the families that are being offered – both the living and the dead for whom we are praying. Frequently, when I receive communion, I say the name of the dead person to indicate that I am receiving on his or her behalf and am asking our Lord to come to the person I am naming.

During the time of the offering of the gifts in communion, sometimes we can picture the person whom God is healing. Seven of us had gathered for a Eucharist service for Dorothy who had suffered from anorexia nervosa for six years. Unknown to Dorothy, we intended to pray for her aborted baby sister and for her father and grandfather, both of whom had committed suicide. Quite suddenly, it seemed to me that a carved black wooden figure of our Lord on the cross appeared on the vast red brick wall behind the altar. I said, 'I thought you, Lord, were above; how is it you are not alive?' There was no answer. Then I heard someone striding noisily up the church aisle and I assumed it was a tourist. Unceremoniously, this person, a girl in her twenties with long fair hair and an ankle-length dress, pushed between our group and the communion table a few inches away. She went up to the cross and the Lord stepped down and drew her into his arms. She remained there, weeping, through the priest's prayers of consecration until near the end of communion. Then the whole scene disappeared.

After the service I asked the priest why he had centred his prayers so much on children while omitting to bring in the two suicides. He responded that, as the service progressed, he had felt that the father and grandfather had received sufficient love so he changed the focus to the aborted baby. Dorothy's mother added abruptly, 'Yes, it was for her I was praying. I had a picture of the Lord and heard that my baby's name was June, so I knew it had been a girl. She would have been born in June.' Then I told them about my picture of the girl coming to the cross and Dorothy's mother said, 'That's right, she sounds just like my other children – noisy, clumsy and fair-haired. My abortion was exactly twenty-one years ago.'

That evening, she travelled to the town where Dorothy was ill in bed. When the girl heard what had happened at the service she said, 'I know her. She has been calling me by name, asking me for help for years, but I never dared to tell anyone because I thought I would have been locked up for hearing voices!' Dorothy and her mother were now at peace. A week later Dorothy, who was eating normally, made a five hundred mile round trip by train to say 'thank you' to us all.

Each of the seven of us experienced that Eucharist differently. The priest felt a strong influence, Dorothy's mother heard a directing voice, and I had a clear vision. The other four people present were supportive and simply prayed that God would act in his most loving way towards Dorothy. What matters most at a Eucharist is not our worrying about what our own experiences will be – feelings, voices or visions – but rather that we concentrate on showing the Lord to the dead person and letting him bring healing to the living. The Eucharist uses all the traditional means to drive out evil: Scripture, prayer in Jesus Christ's name, confession of sin and absolution, profession of faith, the Lord's Prayer, fellowship in worshipping praise, communion, laying on of hands and blessing. Evil spirits fear both the tremendous power for good that this generates and also the way in which the spirit of God can change the hearts of men. The sacrifice of Christ, which he offered without reservation to God for man's redemption, purifies man's conscience so that he is able truly to serve God.

For instance, when Tom saw his real and adoptive parents embracing each other with Mary, he experienced Mary's deep compassion for them and he began to feel love where previously he had felt rejection as an orphan. In Mary, Tom also discovered that he had a very special mother whose love could reach his hurt. If Tom had seen nothing, it is doubtful whether his whole person would have felt healed. Jesus Christ often lets us see what he knows we need to experience in order that his healing may take place.

Each of us came away from the service for Dorothy with a deep love for one another and for Dorothy herself (even though we did not then know that she had been cured), and for our Lord. Such an abundance of love could only have come from God (Gal. 5.22).

Understanding how love emanates from Jesus Christ both for the dead and for the living, and sensing who is present at our services, can help us to focus our prayers properly. At a Eucharist which we held in England for an American lady's schizophrenic son who was institutionalized in America, I learned the power of prayer at a distance, as God draws the dead to himself. At the side of the church, I observed a small dark figure with round shoulders like a hunchback and at first I thought he was an assistant to the priest. Then I saw a vision of our Lord on the right-hand side of the altar looking down at us and saying, 'At last someone is doing something about him.' As our prayers ended, the hunchback seemed to float upwards to join a number of gowned figures who were grouped round the Lord and saying, 'We will look after you.'

Over a cup of coffee after the service, I was describing my vision when suddenly the American woman banged the table hard with her fist. 'That is my father,' she shouted defensively, 'I prayed for him. He was a little hunchback and he committed suicide. I was not going to tell you.' Four days later this mother had a letter from her son in America. His schizophrenia had disappeared. Today, twelve years later, it has not returned. So much can still happen even when the patient is not present and does not know that he or she is being prayed for.

Judy was her father's favourite child. They were both involved in a serious traffic accident abroad when she was eleven years old and she suffered various fractures and severe concussion. For a month she lay in a coma. Eventually regaining consciousness, she was faced with the news that her father had died in the accident. Judy became very depressed, then schizophrenic, and finally was diagnosed as having anorexia nervosa. By her eighteenth birthday she weighed just over five stone.

Between 15 and 30 per cent of patients with anorexia nervosa die from the disease if it is treated by conventional means. Sixty-six such patients have been brought to me over the past few years and fifty-one are now quite well. Five were removed from my care and ten are still unresolved.

Judy's medical records showed that her doctors were already coping adequately with her physical symptoms but, after checking her blood count and enquiring about her diet and sleeping patterns, I prescribed large doses of vitamin B complex to help her waning general alertness and concentration.

During our consultation, Judy's answers to my questions were punctuated with references to her dead father. Three times she said, 'I want to join Daddy', and I learned that, during one of her periods in hospital, she had thought about suicide as a way to do just that. She also gave me the impression that her continuing distress was aggravated by the fact that her father's body had been flown home and cremated rather hastily while her mother and the rest of her family were recovering from the shock of the accident and enduring extreme anxiety as Judy herself lay in a coma, hovering between life and death.

Although we gently explored the Family Tree together, it did not offer a solution, for no other ancestors seemed to be in need of prayer. All of Judy's mental resources and physical energy were focused on her father. When she was able to accept that it was he who needed to be released by her own prayers, she agreed to participate in a Eucharist for him, conducted by her priest. On the morning following the service, Judy's mother began trying to persuade the girl to eat breakfast, expecting the usual refusal. The firm reply, 'Stop fussing over me! I'm hungry!' startled her considerably.

Judy's normal appetite returned and she made radical changes in her life. A spiritual discipline became part of her routine, with quiet times set aside for listening to God and for daily Bible readings, as well as regular participation in the Eucharist at her church. She is now a qualified nurse and finds that her long history of illness has given her greater compassion for her patients.

(iv) The fourth stage

At the final blessing, the fourth healing stage takes place. We shift our focus away from the needs of the dead and pray essentially for the needs of the living. Those present often join silently in this prayer by laying their hands on the heads of those who are especially seeking healing, and the minister may make the sign of the cross (sometimes with oil) on their foreheads, thus focusing the healing of Jesus Christ.

A nineteen-year-old epileptic girl whose right side was paralysed experienced her own healing at the blessing and the laying on of hands following the Eucharist for her dead grandfather. To her, the healing came as a release which started from her shoulders and spread slowly throughout her entire body. After the final prayer she could move normally. She has never had another epileptic fit. By extending our hands over the sick person, we became channels through which Jesus Christ and, perhaps, the dead can express their love.

This expression of love continues each time a Eucharist is held. Many saints such as Elizabeth of Hungary, Teresa of Avila, Thomas Aquinas and St Malachy record the healing power for the living of the Eucharist offered for the dead. St Bernard gives this account of St Malachy's experience: 'The sister of Saint Malachy was so worldly-minded that her brother determined not to see her any more as long as she lived. Although he did not see her in the flesh he was to see her again in spirit. After her death, one night he heard a voice telling him that his sister was at the door, complaining that she had had nothing to eat for thirty days. The saint, when he awoke, forthwith understood what food it was that she needed;

for it was exactly thirty days since he had offered the sacrifice of the Living Bread (the Eucharist of the Resurrection) for her. He began again to give her this benefit, which he had withheld from her. Soon he saw her coming up to the church but she could not yet enter as she was still wearing a black garment. He continued to offer the holy Sacrifice for her every day and soon saw her a second time, dressed in a lighter garment. Finally, he saw her a third time, clad entirely in white, and surrounded by blessed spirits.'

As a result of the repeated Eucharists, both St Malachy and his dead sister received healing. In the hardness of his heart he had determined never to see his sister again and he had needed to be reconciled with her. Through the Eucharist he began to love and forgive and feed her (with the Living Bread) at thirty-day intervals, and, finally, daily. As he became more whole, so did his dead sister. He deeply appreciated the healing power of the Eucharist repeatedly offered for the dead and when asked how he wished to die, he said he hoped it would happen on All Souls' Day (2 November) in St Bernard's monastery, because on that day each year all the monks offered a Eucharist for the departed. In fact, his wish was granted and St Malachy died in St Bernard's monastery on 2 November while stopping there en route for Rome.

It is sometimes necessary to repeat the Eucharist several times before it is evident that its healing work is done. During the Summer of 1978 the importance of such repetition was made clear to me. While I was in the United States, a bishop of the American Episcopal Church brought one of his priests to see me. For forty years the man had suffered from stuttering and slurred speech and had lost many appointments because of his disability. No medical treatment had helped him. Also, he had two red marks running vertically down the front of his neck, which frequently bled, and an eczematous rash on his face and around his abdomen.

On enquiring into his Family Tree, I found that the priest's favourite brother had committed suicide and there were also two abortions and two miscarriages in his immediate ancestry. We held a Eucharist for them and when the man placed his Family Tree on the altar at the offering of gifts, I sensed the Lord and his angels above us. In front of him knelt two veiled women. I asked, 'Lord, why not four people?' He answered, 'These two women are the abortions.' I also saw two angels dragging along a man who was trying to resist and they forced him to look at the offerings of bread and wine. At the end of the service, he was taken off to the right, but the angels lifted up the two women into a bright light on the left, where the Lord had been, and from that bright light a vast array of people reached down to welcome them. The Lord said, 'This is their family; the miscarriages are there already.'

That afternoon I talked over the service with the priest's relative who had had the miscarriages. 'I know why they are already in heaven,' she said. 'It is because I have always prayed for them and loved them.'

It was only after the seventh morning service that the unwilling man, who had committed suicide, was taken at last into the light. Since then the afflicted priest has been released from his physical symptoms of eczema and bleeding marks and almost completely cured of his disturbed speech. His improvement enabled him to secure full-time work in the ministry and, a year later, his speech was almost normal as he celebrated a Eucharist for some other patients of mine.

Although, in my experience only one Eucharist is usually required to release a lost baby, repeated services may be necessary to release an adult in more need of love and forgiveness. I do not think that the Lord demands a certain magical number of Eucharists.[1] It depends upon how much love the dead person needs and how much the living are able to give. The deeper the wound, the more love is needed. This can be given in one Eucharist prayed with deep love or a hundred Eucharists prayed routinely. It may be that even after a lost baby or adult has been released, further Eucharists can draw them more deeply into Jesus' care. 'In my Father's house are many rooms' (John 14.2). Perhaps these open to us in proportion to the depth of our knowledge of Jesus' love. As our love grows we shall come to the Eucharist asking Jesus Christ, 'How do you want to love through me today?' Often he will not wish us to focus on the dead but will lead us to pray for someone who is sick or burdened, to forgive an insensitive friend, to ask for guidance on how to reach out to a poor neighbour or simply to praise and thank the Father for his generosity. There are as many ways of praying at the Eucharist as there are ways of loving and receiving love.

Jesus Christ did not pray in this way for people when he was alive because there was as yet no resurrection, but he promised that 'anyone who has faith in me . . . will do even greater things than these, because I am going to the Father' (John 14.12). When Jesus ascended he opened the gates of heaven. He was 'the first fruits of those who have fallen asleep' (1 Cor. 15.20).

4

Freedom to Choose

Jesus' first Eucharist did not heal a Judas who betrayed his Lord or a Peter who denied him. The Eucharist simply gives Jesus' life, and we have the choice between living out this life or rejecting it. Peter's struggle to live out Jesus' life taught him the importance of being with supportive Christian friends who devoted themselves 'to the fellowship, to the breaking of bread, and to prayer' (Acts 2.42). On many occasions my home has provided a haven for various struggling people so that they could live in a similar Christian supportive atmosphere in order to strengthen their healings. We need Jesus both in the Eucharist and in one another, as Joe discovered.

From childhood, Joe had been trained to be a member of a gang of burglars, graduating to become the trusted driver for the raids. He had handled stolen property worth £700,000 but was thirty-eight years old before the police finally caught him stealing paintings from a well-known artist's studio. He was sent to prison for three years and during this time the artist made a point of visiting him every week. When Joe was released, the artist met him at the prison gate and took him to his own home. There, Joe experienced trust and love for the first time in his life.

After staying for some time with the man he had robbed, Joe came to live with my family. We continued to look after him and to build him up in body, mind and soul through our daily pattern of life. He thrived on the regular exercise of gardening or sawing wood and he relaxed in the beautiful surroundings of the countryside. Many people expect mental and physical healing to come to them without their having to change to a balanced way of life with exercise, healthy diet, proper rest and recreation.

Every morning, Joe and I made a quiet time alone with God and sought his guidance for the day. When Joe first began to do this, he went through a difficult period during which he remembered all the various caches of loot. With police co-operation, he made some restitution but the police were naturally suspicious and constantly watched him, often suspecting him when another burglary was committed. Joe first had to accept God's forgiveness; then forgive himself and the police, and also try to help those whom he had hurt. I have seen other people in similar circumstances remain mentally ill because they could not forgive themselves or another person, a lesson which Joe learned through the essential support of his friends.

It is vitally important to help a person like Joe take responsibility for his own actions and to make reparation to those he has harmed. Doctor Karl Menninger in his book *Whatever Became of Sin?*, affirms that it is healthy to say, 'I am a sinner – one who is responsible for my evil actions but who, with God's help, can change.' The dependent personality, however, will not want to admit he has power to change but will continue to blame his evil actions on outside control, maintaining that 'the devil or an ancestor made me do it'.

To allow a person to use this prop as an excuse for evading responsibility where he has the freedom to change merely reinforces the evil. One should be wary of blaming such outside controls especially if the person is failing to develop and to utilize to the full his remaining freedom. The ideal attitude is that of Molly, the lady with a fear of water related to her uncle's drowning in the *Titanic* disaster (Chapter 2). With God's help she dispelled 'this new and ridiculous phobia'. Not all patients feel that they can command sufficient strength and freedom of choice to make such a strong statement, but most of them, with help, can be brought to acknowledge and use whatever freedom they still have.

Release from control by the spirit world is somewhat similar to release from control by alcohol. Some current theories suggest that an alcoholic lacks an enzyme for converting alcohol in the body and that this deficiency may have a genetic origin going back for generations. From the time when the body stops producing the enzyme, an alcoholic loses his basic willpower to stop drinking and is unable to do so without help. Similarly, those who are under the control of the spirit world suffer from a spiritual illness as real as alcoholism. It may have a genetic origin going back for generations and even altering the physical make-up to cause both physical and emotional illnesses. The patient eventually has no freedom of will and is driven in the same way as an alcoholic. It does little good to demand the exercise of greater willpower; he needs help.

An alcoholic's recovery often results from following a programme such as that produced by Alcoholics Anonymous. This places the emphasis not on willpower alone but on a higher power and a helpful community which encourage the alcoholic to take responsibility for using his freedom to give up alcohol for the rest of his life. So too, release from control by the spirit world relies on the higher power of our Lord and the follow-up in the Christian community that encourages a person to utilize and expand his growing freedom. As an alcoholic experiences a new freedom when he is dried out, so a person suffering from spirit control experiences new freedom after a Eucharist or other prayers for his release. In each case, there will be a strong temptation to revert to the old habits rather than to continue to use the new freedom. Many will be convinced, wrongly, that they can continue to reform solely by their own willpower and without God or the help of a community.

To help alcoholics through this critical period, the Alcoholics Anonymous programme focuses on twelve steps – steps which are equally essential for breaking bondage to the spirit world. Joe and many other patients who have stayed free from their parallel bondage to the spirit world have managed to do so because they have continued to follow these twelve steps.

1. We admitted we were powerless over alcohol and that our lives had become unmanageable.
2. We came to believe that a Power greater than ourselves could restore us to sanity.
3. We made a decision to turn our will and our lives over to the care of God as we understood him.
4. We made a searching and fearless moral inventory of ourselves.
5. We admitted to God, to ourselves, and to another human being the exact nature of our wrongs.
6. We were entirely ready to allow God to remove all these defects of character.

7. We humbly ask him to remove our shortcomings.

8. We made a list of all persons we had harmed, and became willing to make amends to all.

9. We made direct amends to such people wherever possible, except when to do so would injure them or others.

10. We continued to take personal inventory and when we were wrong, promptly admitted it.

11. We sought through prayer and meditation to improve our conscious contact with God as we understood him, praying only for knowledge of his will for us and the power to carry that out.

12. Having had a spiritual awakening as the result of these steps, we tried to carry this message to alcoholics, and to practise these principles in all our affairs.

It should be noted that this programme leads up to the final step of a spiritual awakening so strong that a reformed alcoholic can help another alcoholic. Similarly, as patients are freed from spirit control they find that their spiritual awakening leads them to free others through prayer and especially through participating in the Eucharist.

Sometimes, it seems that the Lord calls us to extend our prayers beyond our own family or friends. Manya began the Eucharist by praying for three of her Polish-Jewish relations. She was astonished to find that they brought with them hundreds of dishevelled Polish Jews, heads lowered, filing out of concentration camps and shuffling towards the altar. When Manya was about to walk up the aisle to receive the Eucharist, she felt impeded because it seemed to her that all the aisles were jammed with these refugees. As she continued to pray, Manya saw Jesus standing at the altar waiting to welcome them. They approached and looked up at him and then started to dance and sing hallelujahs as the angels led them up into a bright light behind the altar.

Even after the service was over, more refugees continued to stream up the aisle. Manya and several other people stayed in the church praying for all Jewish people although there had been no mention of Jews. They saw many of them being set free at the altar. Manya's husband, a minister, shared in this very real experience and was so much affected by it that he called together his congregation and held a Eucharist of the Resurrection when he returned home. He had witnessed how Jesus frees and releases those who come to him not only during the Eucharist but even outside it. Thus, Jesus asks us to continue to love the dead for whom we have prayed, both during and after the Eucharist.

Of course, we should continue to pray for the living as well. Sometimes our prayers do not seem to be answered and the living do not appear to benefit from them. At such times I want to ask God, 'Why are you not helping this person?' One can identify many reasons why a person does not receive healing: he will not give himself totally to Jesus, he will not forgive, or he will not live a balanced life. On the other hand, it must be said that some people are healed who do not do any of these things. Often the fundamental cause is lack of supportive love in the Christian community, but sometimes it is simply that we are not listening closely enough to hear God's plan which is unique for each individual. Although a person may not seem to be receiving help in the way we envisage, we are assured that our prayers are never wasted (Rom. 8.26).

When I pray at the Eucharist, although I cannot be sure what will happen, I know that my prayer will be answered in a loving way. I believe that even when the Lord is not ostensibly healing in the way that I think is needed, he is using my prayer to heal in a different way – perhaps, for a person whom I may never see. He may be healing the person who has come to pray at the Eucharist, that is the celebrant, or it may be one of the most important people in the church hierarchy such as a bishop or, as we have found at numerous services, perhaps it may be a forgotten relative who is healed and released from a hospital in another country. We must be ready to listen to God's directive as we ask him to reveal his next immediate healing step.

An elderly woman, Josephine, suffered from a disease of senility which left her with irreversible scarring of the brain. We held a Eucharist for her and we were disappointed when no healing seemed to occur. Beyond our knowledge, the Lord was taking the next immediate step in healing through Josephine's brother, who was a priest. During the Eucharist for his sister he experienced a deep love and sense of compassion that brought him closer, not only to her but to all mentally disturbed people. As a direct result, he now spends a day every week visiting them and praying with them for healing and his Christian ministry has been immeasurably enriched.

Once, when I was in New York, I attended a Eucharist with a woman who was hearing voices and practising automatic writing. I expected that, as we prayed, she would be freed from this spirit control, and indeed the voices ceased during the Eucharist. Two days later they returned.

Eventually, some friends took her to see a bishop who, with some reluctance said a prayer of deliverance for her. She was completely and permanently freed from her possession. And the bishop, through his own deliverance prayer suddenly discovered the power of the evil one and the greater reality and extent of Jesus' healing power. So we witnessed the Lord working out his total plan for both the complete healing of the woman and the revelation to the bishop.

One of the most dramatic healings of my career happened with Claudine. She was fifty years old and had spent twelve years under constant supervision in hospital, suffering from chronic schizophrenia. Neither treatments nor drugs had affected her violent temper which was coupled with a delusional state of mind. Her doctors felt that there was nothing to lose – she could not deteriorate any further – and a decision was taken to operate on her brain in a London hospital.

The operation failed. Claudine did deteriorate further, losing the power of both sight and speech. With this irreversible damage and with no change in her schizo-phrenic state, Claudine was given up and left to 'vegetate' in a mental hospital. She became corpulent which combined with her baldness (no hair had grown on her head since her operation), gave her a rather repulsive appearance. About eighteen months later her family obtained permission from the institution in which Claudine lived for her to spend a day and a night at home.

She was brought to me. She gave no indication of under-standing anything that was said to her and, after a quick check-up, I confirmed that there seemed to be no hope for her and I could recommend no therapy. The damage was indeed irreversible. At that time, I did not understand the influence of the Family Tree nor even realize the extent of the healing power of the Eucharist. Not knowing what else to say or do, I prayed aloud, simply trying to listen for the Lord's guidance and seeking his forgiveness for man's destruction of a human being. Then we said the Lord's Prayer together with its final plea, 'Deliver us from evil'. Our prayer was that Claudine might be left in peace. My patient and her family returned to their own home where she was to remain overnight.

Next morning, the whole household was awakened by Claudine shouting, 'Come and look at me!' Not having heard a word from Claudine since her disastrous operation, her startled parents rushed into the room. Claudine was gazing at her reflection in the mirror and shouting, 'Look at my hair!' During the night, a quarter-inch of hair had appeared all over her head. She could speak, she could see, she could grow!

Later that day, Claudine was taken back to the institution. Astonished by the change in her, doctors questioned her for several hours. Repeatedly she explained simply, 'They prayed with me.' The doctors could not understand what had happened. It was almost beyond belief that a patient who had suffered such total disabilities could be healed so suddenly and so completely that she could be readmitted to the normal world outside.

When I was first confronted by Claudine, I had tried to listen to God, but I heard no voice and recognized no clear guidance. I felt only compassion for Claudine and anger and resentment at the ineptitude of those who had almost destroyed her. Jesus, confronted by a leper, was filled with compassion for the sufferer (Mark 1.41), and the more we can identify with the feelings of Jesus towards a person, the greater is the degree to which we are able to do his will on behalf of that person. The core of our thinking as we draw up Family Trees for the Eucharist must be an active, ever-present readiness to listen so that we may become more aware of our Lord taking his next immediate steps (Gal. 2.20).

While I was at university another student introduced me to the art of listening. He was a nuisance. His insistence that I should learn to listen to God's voice became so intensely irritating to me that, eventually, in order to close the subject, I agreed to sit with him in silence for half an hour in my room. At the end of the time, he asked me what I was thinking. 'Nothing,' I told him. 'Did God speak to you?' he enquired hopefully. 'Of course not,' I snapped. 'You can't make your mind a complete blank,' he argued. 'What did you think about?' I told him that I had just been looking at the titles on my bookshelf.

'That's interesting,' he said. 'Read them to me.' Bored and wanting to end the session, I read out the names on the spines of several of the books and then gave up. 'You haven't finished,' urged my friend. I named a few more titles. 'Go on, there are still three more books,' he said quickly. Curtly, I answered, 'I've finished with them.' 'Well then, sell them!' he shot back. Finally, I confessed that long ago, I had borrowed the books from my old school and had never returned them. My friend persuaded me to put the situation right so I wrote a letter of apology, parcelled up the three books and, under his escort, took them straight to the post office. Strangely, I felt as free as air, as though a burden I had been carrying was no longer there.

In those days I was not sure what I was listening to, but throughout my life God has spoken to me many times, directing my thoughts and actions. 'He wakens me morning by morning, wakens my ear to listen like one being taught' (Isa. 50.4).

One morning when I awakened, I found myself thinking of the then Prime Minister, a man I had never met. I had an intense image about a personal decision he had to make and I felt an urgency to send him a warning about his intended course of action. Although it seemed presumptuous on my part, I wrote a letter to him explaining the situation. Some weeks later, there came a reply in which he thanked me for my intervention which had prevented him from taking an irrevocable and erroneous step.

Once, in the half-awake, half-dreaming world of early morning, I had an image of a friend called Mabel whom we had not seen for eight years. In the 'dream' she was yelling out of the third floor window of a strange brick building. This meant nothing to me at the time but I scribbled the name Mabel on a piece of paper and forgot about it.

That same evening, as I was driving home from work, I was held up at a traffic light. As my frustration and impatience grew I felt the Lord was directing me to turn left. I argued, 'No, I want to go straight home.' 'Turn left,' he commanded. I was alone; the alternative route would add only five minutes to my journey. I turned left. Feeling rather foolish, I nevertheless drove very slowly so as not to miss anything. Then from the right-hand side of the road a woman's voice shouted, 'Doctor Ken! Doctor Ken!' I glanced up. Our friend Mabel was leaning out of the identical third floor window of my 'half-dream' that morning. By the time I had parked my car and climbed three long flights of stairs, I knew that this was no dream.

Mabel explained. Early that morning, she had come to this block of flats to collect her sister because they had just heard that their older brother, who had lung cancer, was dying. Many years before, I had treated their brother, so the sisters had spent the day trying to contact me. This incident proved to me that one of the most important aspects of early morning listening to God is the fostering of an attitude of continual listening throughout the day – even at a frustrating red traffic light. Otherwise, I would not have been receptive to the direction of the Lord when he was showing me the conclusion of my 'half-dream', and I would not have found Mabel when she needed me, as he required me to do. The psychiatrist William James commented, 'We and God have business together; in opening ourselves to his influence our deepest destiny is fulfilled. God is real because he produces real effects.'

On another occasion the promptings of God's voice enabled me to offer some advice which probably saved many lives. I was visiting some friends in Texas, and chatted one day to a neighbour who happened to work at NASA (National Aeronautics and Space Administration). When he discovered something of my background, and learned that I was a psychiatrist who had been imprisoned for a long period in China, and that one of my hobbies is painting, he told me delightedly that I was 'just the person they were looking for'.

Taken by surprise, I agreed to accompany him to the plant. Apparently, there was an urgent need for advice on an important detail of a projected space station. The planners appreciated that harmonious interior decorations would be of considerable help to the men who would have to look at the same walls, patterns and colours in a confined area over a long period of time. Therefore, they wanted to consult someone who understood the psychological effects of various colours and designs, preferably someone who had been similarly confined. I was pleased to help and made many suggestions for the space shuttle and skylab.

I was privileged to watch the Moonrover undergoing test drives and to ask questions. On being told that the tyres were filled with nitrogen I heard the Lord's voice saying, 'Those men will be in danger!' I discussed this with the Director who was accompanying me, who explained that the experts had realized the obvious consequences if a tyre were to puncture. However, after fourteen years of research, they considered this to be a very remote possibility. Silently I put the problem to the Lord and, under his guidance, drew a sketch on a slip of paper of wheels with coiled springs connecting the axle to a perforated metal strip which would act as a tyre. The Director looked at my drawing, laughed and put it into his pocket.

Four months later, one of the television commentators who was covering the moon landing mentioned that, at the last moment, the Goodyear nitrogen-inflated tyres had been converted to coiled spring wheels! Enquiring about this from the neighbour who had introduced me to the NASA establishment, I was not surprised to be told, 'It was very strange. The Director simply found a drawing in his pocket and knew that a change should be made in the construction of the wheels. He was not sure where the paper came from.' I was sure. Once again, God had used me to produce a 'real effect' for I was told in 1979 that those wheels had saved men's lives.

5

'Suffer the little children . . .'

We have no difficulty in believing that our prayers help the living through Jesus Christ's intercession (1 Tim. 2.1–4). Indeed, we know we are following his example when he prayed for us all, even with the shadow of the cross upon him (John 17).

In the Christian church we take innocent, new-born babies, who do not seem to need prayer, and baptize them in order to give them the prayerful support of a Christian community. Some people feel that even baptized babies need a prayer to exorcise them from the evil which they may have encountered while still in the womb. It seems to them that any child who has experienced moments of hurt should have the benefit of healing prayer. It is natural that unloving memories need to be healed and this can be done through the love of Jesus at the Eucharist. Just as baptism allows babies to be brought into the community of the church, so it is possible that the death and resurrection of Jesus, celebrated in the Eucharist, can touch those babies who have not been baptized.

Medical studies have shown how stress or the taking of drugs, nicotine or alcohol by the mother can affect the fetus detrimentally.[1] The unborn child can absorb thoughts and feelings as well as toxic substances.[2] I find it is reasonable therefore to suppose that it can also absorb prayer.

An experiment conducted by Dr J. Cowdy at a Salisbury hospital in 1958 showed that from about fourteen weeks a fetus will have formed a memory area in the brain into which emotions and sounds coming from its parents are recorded. This can be proved and the information retrieved in adult life by the technique known as drug abreaction – the intravenous injection of a diluted anaesthetic commonly called the truth drug. Under such treatment one disturbed patient recalled her father's comment before she was born: 'I'll wring the baby's neck, if it is a girl!' He had actually said those words. Eventually, she came to terms with this inborn hurt and was released from hospital.

A study presented in 1978 at Loyola University, Chicago, found that some patients attempted suicide every year on the same date. Investigating this phenomenon Andrew Feldmar, a clinical psychologist at Vancouver, deduced that these dates seemed not to relate to holidays, family deaths, or other major events, but that they coincided with the dates on which their mothers had tried to abort them. Even the method of attempted suicide which they used (poisoning, stabbing by sharp instruments, etc.) corresponded to the method that had been tried in the attempted abortion. Feldmar was further surprised to find that the fetus had absorbed the knowledge of abortion attempts even when they occurred during the first few weeks of pregnancy. He postulated that memory could date from the time when the egg and the sperm united, i.e. from the moment of conception. Such research showed that the fetus may already record memories even before the brain is formed at fourteen weeks.[3]

Similarly, memories of being loved are recorded by the unborn baby. A woman who is at least five months pregnant can perform a test on herself to prove her baby's response to her love. When she places her right hand on the right side of her abdomen and her left hand on the left side, she can actually make her baby move to either hand. To do this, she simply imagines the baby under her right hand growing in strength and goodness while being caressed by her touch. It will move to place its rounded back in the hollow of its mother's loving hand. If the mother then switches her loving concentration from the right hand to the left hand, the child will even move to do the same under the left hand. If the mother does this little exercise daily on a regular time schedule, the child will kick if his 'love bath' is not forthcoming. Thus, not just the violence of attempted abortions but also the simple withdrawal of love affects a fetus.

I have over six hundred recorded cases of direct healing which have taken place after a Eucharist has been celebrated for babies – who were either aborted, miscarried, stillborn or discarded at birth and who had never been loved or properly committed to Jesus Christ in a burial service. When a Eucharist has been held for such infants, the results have been startling. Many have felt the benefit of the healing power that was generated including patients who were actually taking part; patients who were miles away in hospitals and mental institutions and knew nothing about the services; and even disturbed relatives in foreign countries.

First, it is essential to establish that the correct medical diagnosis has been made. While this may have been done successfully and the relevant treatment given, I often discover that no account has been taken of the patients' mental state and no attempt has been made to uncover patterns behind unacceptable emotional behaviour. Since irrational states are often the result of varying degrees of pressure exerted by the possession syndrome, an enquiry into the family background is the next step. We draw up as complete a Family Tree as possible. By doing this the cause of trouble may be uncovered and the identification of the uncommitted resolved. People forget, or deliberately hide, unpleasant past happenings and often find it traumatic to be brought face to face with them.

Such patients have been referred to me with various diagnoses, including schizophrenics, epileptics, depressives of every classification, attempted suicides, neurotics, hysterics and several cases of anorexia nervosa. Their behaviour patterns ran the whole gamut of psychiatric illness – acting out paranoid fantasies, hearing voices, being Jesus Christ, acting with brutality or curling up in bed sucking a thumb. Their physical illnesses ranged from migraine to arthritis in the feet. Many had the typically dependent institutional personality which results from countless spells in hospitals. Some were near death; others imagined they were.

Joan was referred to me by a general practitioner colleague. Before my first appointment with the nine-year-old child I studied the notes from her team of hospital doctors and the reports from her headmistress. At the age of five Joan's sunny disposition changed suddenly. She became difficult to cope with and irrational in her behaviour and she was finally diagnosed as an epileptic. Her mother was frightened and puzzled. She wrote to me, 'When Joan goes into one of these states, her face becomes distorted and she will scream at me for minutes on end. She is so far from being her normal self that it makes me cold. The only way of dealing with the worst of these attacks is by prayer and then, after struggling and fighting even harder, she suddenly breaks down, comes willingly into my arms and sobs like a toddler. I feel completely inadequate to deal with her, and that is why we were wondering if we might come to see you.'

The child's headmistress shared this concern. She wrote, 'Joan easily loses her self-control and is given to outbursts of emotion. Her presentation of work leaves much to be desired and, even when copying, she makes innumerable mistakes – probably due to her inability to concentrate for more than a little while.'

As I talked with Joan's parents, I searched for a pattern to her behaviour but could not find one. They told me how the 'attacks' had started suddenly when Joan, then aged five, had fallen unconscious for no apparent reason. Many times since then she had injured herself and once she had split open her chin. Recently, she had begun running out in front of cars so her parents had to restrain her with reins for her own safety. Her father described how she would fight with the strength of an ox and would scream at him, 'I hate you. You are not my daddy. Why was I ever born?' He also feared for the family's safety since, in one of her irrational moods, Joan had threatened her brother with a knife demanding, 'Tell me who you are!' With just as much insistence she shouted, 'I am not Joan.'

From the medical records it seemed to me that the doctors were doing all they could to help Joan in terms of diet, drugs and other therapy. When we began to draw up the Family Tree, I explained that I was especially interested in discovering any one of the ancestors who had not had a proper burial service, and who had died without being committed to Jesus Christ – for example, suicides. I seemed to have no success. From Joan's Family Tree, it was apparent that, for the past four generations at least, there had been no such omission.

Then we called Joan into the room. She came immediately and sat on my knee and I asked her how many brothers and sisters she had. Her reply surprised me. 'I have three brothers and three sisters,' she said. 'But Joan,' I queried, 'your mother says you have three brothers and only two sisters.' Joan became extremely angry, jumped from my knee and stamped about, shouting, 'I have three sisters, not two! Do you see that woman sitting over there?' she screamed, pointing at her mother. 'She is a murderer. She flushed my sister away down the toilet. My sister is a friend of mine. I know her. She's called Melissa.' Joan's accused mother burst into tears and shouted, 'Look out! She is going to have a fit!' Joan's father became red in the face and began to remonstrate with his wife. As they argued, I held Joan tight and said, 'Let's just you and I pray to Jesus and ask him to look after Melissa.' So we prayed, 'Dear Lord Jesus, please look after Melissa and take her into your kingdom.'

It was obvious that Joan had hit a sore spot with her parents. Some time later, her mother told me she had had an accidental abortion through a doctor's rough handling before Joan was born. She had not mentioned it when we drew up the Family Tree because her husband Graham had always denied that his wife had been pregnant on that occasion. At the time of the miscarriage they had been on a holiday to help him to recover from a nervous breakdown, and Joan's mother felt that her husband was in too fragile a state to be forced to face the situation with her. She had never mentioned the incident to Joan and no one knew the name she had wanted for the baby – Melissa.

Since our spirit can be attentive to those who have died without being lovingly committed to Jesus Christ, it was not at all surprising that Joan knew about Melissa. Indeed, I had about 1,400 similar cases in my files. It seemed obvious that this uncommitted baby was the cause of Joan's difficulties and, perhaps, of the troublesome migraines from which her mother had suffered for years. So we held a Eucharist for Melissa and the results changed that family's life. Joan's emotional outbursts, irrational behaviour and even her inability to concentrate all disappeared, never to return. Tests proved that her epilepsy was cured and shortly afterwards she was taken off all drugs. Her mother's migraines were a thing of the past.

But the family's troubles were not yet completely over. Some months later, just before Christmas, Graham collapsed at his work. His symptoms were typical of a 'workaholic' breakdown. He felt he was a terrible and total failure; he was unable to return to his job and was sure he would never work again. After months of medication, his blood pressure remained alarmingly high and his own doctor sent him to me. Naturally, I assumed that he had not come to terms with what had been the root cause of Joan's problems and so had not released his baby Melissa. He denied this suggestion but he thought he knew the reason for his illness. He told me, 'My problem is not Melissa, it is my mother. She was a rather formal, Victorian type of person and very possessive. She never accepted my marriage and she did not like my wife. When she died, I hated her so much that I refused to go to her funeral.' I needed to say no more. Recalling the healing of his daughter Joan, Graham and his family gladly attended a Eucharist for his mother. Within a week, his blood pressure had dropped to normal and he was soon able to go back to work.

Now Graham's concern is not confined to his own family: he and his wife have used their spiritual freedom to reach out to others. The last note I received from Joan's mother was very different from the anxious, helpless one she had first sent to me about her daughter. 'Yesterday Graham and I went to a meeting at the local hospital arranged by the children's department for parents of children who have fits, convulsions or epilepsy. It was not because of Joan that we felt we needed to go, for the Lord has been so good to her. We both thought we might be useful because of our experience. They have our phone number if any parent wants someone to talk to.'

Graham and his wife are doing more than giving out their telephone number. The letter went on to tell me that Graham had been praying in one of the wards at the hospital for a baby with epilepsy and gastro-enteritis. 'Afterwards, I felt that I just had to kiss the baby's mother, which is something I would not have done until I went through all this with Joan. I didn't really know the lady very well but it was just the right thing to do because she flung her arms around me and clung to me for support.' Joan and Graham, like so many others, have found new strength to act with new freedom. A year later, Joan is a happy, healthy little girl, doing extremely well at school and is the joy of her family. Graham remains fit and stable, taking family prayers every evening and he and his wife are most willing to share their experience with anyone who might be helped by hearing about it.

The people most often affected by uncommitted babies who need prayer and who, therefore, are most likely to suffer from various physical or emotional problems are the parents, a twin, the next-born child, a child adopted in its place or even, as in Joan's case, the most sensitive child in the family. Sometimes parents will not be troubled by such events in their past until they experience the reality of prayer. A local vicar saw for himself that one of his parishioners had been healed from a seemingly incurable mental condition and released from hospital after she had prayed for her aborted baby and brought it to the Lord at a Eucharist. The vicar, much encouraged, went to visit another of his parishioners, Mildred, a woman in her sixties who had been undergoing hospital treatment for two years because of her stomach ailments. No medical cause could be found, but her painful symptoms continued. After some discussion, the vicar persuaded Mildred to draw up a Family Tree to establish whether any of her ancestors had died without a loving committal. They could find none.

Suddenly Mildred said, 'All right, I will tell you what I have never told anyone in my life. When I was a teenager, I had an abortion. I have never done anything about it at all.' The vicar suggested that they should hold a service in the church to commit her aborted child to God's keeping and she agreed. By the time the service ended, all her stomach pains had vanished and she felt a tremendous sense of release and joy. She wanted to tell everyone that her whole life had changed.

I asked the vicar why it was only two years earlier that Mildred's stomach problems had begun when the abortion had happened many years before. He told me that it was two years ago that she had decided to become a Christian and join the church, so it was only in the last two years that she had learned to pray. It would seem that her child, having spiritual access to her at last, had tried to attract her attention through that pain in her stomach. It was almost as though the child was being the stomach ache.

Perhaps the vicar's interpretation was right. Illnesses such as severe stomach problems tend to keep us focused on ourselves and make it difficult for us to understand the help which the dead person needs. Perhaps such illnesses are the work of the evil one distracting us from prayer. It is more probable that there is a simpler, natural, accurate explanation. When Mildred became a Christian, she took on a new set of moral beliefs and perhaps for the first time she felt guilty about her aborted child. This guilt or inner turmoil may have expressed itself through an upset stomach, for mental trauma often finds physical expression. I am certain that, whether suffering is caused by natural guilt, by a dead person or by the evil one, the Eucharist usually brings healing.[4]

Twins in particular have a special sensitivity to their dead brother or sister. At one Eucharist, a mother mentioned that one of her twin daughters had died at birth, and had been disposed of in the hospital. When this incident was first prayed about it brought tears of rejoicing to the living twin. She said she had 'watched' her twin sister growing up all through the years but had never dared to talk about it.

In India, one summer, a worried mother came to consult me about her schizophrenic daughter who had been in hospital many times. Among other symptoms, she suffered from delusions of grandeur! When we drew up the Family Tree, I discovered that several abortions had been performed within the family. We prayed together about these on two occasions and each time the mother, though a Hindu, said that she saw the feet of Christ on the cross. The following week her daughter travelled six hundred miles to tell her that suddenly she had felt quite well and that all of her symptoms had disappeared. When we told her about our prayers for her, she was very thankful and asked if I could take her to see the Eucharist! After the service the mother, who had again seen Jesus Christ there, decided that she was a fulfilled Hindu.

Sometimes abnormal or antisocial behaviour will occur in a child adopted in place of a lost baby. The problem of a man aged twenty-eight was referred to me by a police-man friend. The man was in prison after his fifteenth arrest for stealing. Even as a child he had stolen from his mother's purse, but strangely he always stole for somebody else and never for his own profit.

Discussing his history with his parents, I asked about his Family Tree. 'He has no Family Tree that we know of,' they said, 'because we adopted him when he was born. After our son died at birth, we went straight to a baby home and adopted a little baby boy who, we thought, looked like our own. We have loved him and looked after him through the years just as if he were our own.' At a Eucharist, these bewildered parents gave a name to their son who had died at birth and released him in prayer to Jesus Christ. Their adopted son left prison a reformed man and now holds a responsible job.

Just as we lovingly name our own children at baptism, we should also name a 'lost' child to express how it belongs to us and is loved. Sometimes a mother or a brother or sister will know the intended name of such a baby; at other times the Lord gives a name as we pray. At one service for a premature baby boy who lived for only four hours and never had a funeral service, the baby's mother was bravely trying to thank Jesus Christ for taking her little son home. She clearly heard his reply. 'No. First you must give him a name and show him that he has a mother's love and then commit him to me.'

A lady diagnosed as a disturbed endogenous (self-engendered) depressive who could neither sleep, eat nor relate to others was referred to me by her doctor. As a young woman, she had been a prostitute and, consequently, had had several miscarriages and abortions. Carefully, she named them, accepted God's forgiveness, and faithfully continued to give them all to the Lord every Sunday when she went to church. She was freed from her depression and has since happily married and is now able to help many other women in similar circumstances.

Releasing 'lost' babies in this way can bring both emotional and physical healing. Two women who had attended a Eucharist for the release of their babies later told me about their physical healing. The first, who remembered two early miscarriages in her prayers, found to her amazement that her pains and symptoms of spinal osteoporosis (a disease in which the bone becomes rarefied) suddenly disappeared. She rose up from her wheelchair and walked out of the church. The other lady remembered and prayed for her own aborted baby and committed it to Jesus Christ. Four days later her doctor reported that she was cured of a chronic colitis.

The Lancasters came to see me much concerned about three of their five children. The eldest child was a drug addict, her sister was grossly overweight and the youngest child had been a thief since the age of seven. During questioning, it emerged that three of the mother's pregnancies had gone awry and Elizabeth, the eldest child, was born after an earlier abortion; Evelyn following a miscarriage, while Charles, the youngest, was adopted to replace a stillborn child. Since these three babies had never been committed to the Lord in any manner, we celebrated a Eucharist for them after which the whole family felt released. Elizabeth never touched drugs again; Charles stopped stealing, and Evelyn's weight returned to normal within three months.

Nowadays, an abortion is a commonplace happening. Nevertheless, the immediate psychological damage to the mother is profound while the long-term effects may last a lifetime.

'People were also bringing babies to Jesus to have him touch them. When the disciples saw this they rebuked them. But Jesus called the children to him and said, "Let the little children come to me, and do not hinder them, for the Kingdom of God belongs to such as these"' (Luke 18.15–16).

Some people believe that all babies go straight to God when they die. This is indeed so if they have been loved and prayed for on earth. I have witnessed over six hundred cases of babies who had died continuing to grow up at the same rate as they would have grown in life. Each baby has its own guardian angel waiting for a time of love and committal to God; the angel then has permission to act. And I disagree with those who argue that if a pregnancy has lasted for only a few weeks the baby was not formed and did not count. My experience of 'seeing' these babies in their own age group proves to me the truth of God's word, 'Before I formed you in the womb I knew you' (Jer. 1.5 and Psalm 139.13). Such babies were real people with souls and memories of the loving God who had once handled them.[5]

6

Laying the Ghost

———•◦•———

Centuries-old traditions call for blessings on buildings and places to rid them of the influences of the dead. I have sixty-five recorded cases of 'hauntings' that have ceased through prayer. They are not the common subjective hauntings seen only by one person and probably caused by the psychological projection of denied experience or by a fertile imagination. These have a note of objectivity – that is, happenings observed by other stable people and objects being moved without human volition. Having considered all possible explanations – mass hallucinations by psychic contagion, occult involvement, or psychiatric imbalance – it seems clear that for many people there is a simple explanation. The ghost which is haunting a place may be a dead person needing prayer. If it is treated as such, I have never found an objective haunting to continue.

It is not only houses and other buildings that can be freed by this prayer formula. It also works for places which are prone to unusual and otherwise inexplicable accidents such as straight stretches of a particular road or areas of the sky or sea like the much-feared Bermuda Triangle.

For hundreds of years the Bermuda Triangle (an area of the Atlantic Ocean enclosed by an imaginary line from Bermuda to Miami to Puerto Rico to Bermuda) has swallowed up ships and aircraft, often without a trace. The sheer weight of the books written on this subject would sink a small ship. Most sailors prefer to avoid the place but, like many other people, especially landlubbers, I scoffed at such irrational fears. In 1972, my wife and I were sailing through the 'triangle' on a banana boat when we were caught in a force 9 storm. We headed south away from the storm into the infamous Sargasso Sea. There, one of the ship's boilers burst, leaving us silently drifting.

In the quietness my wife and I both distinctly heard a strange sound, like a steady droning dirge which continued throughout the day and night. At first we thought it was the Jamaican crew, but after checking we realized that they were not responsible. Then I found a magazine containing diagrams of the old slave ships which used this run, with details of how almost two million slaves were thrown overboard. Arthur Hailey's book *Roots*, recently dramatized on television, told movingly of the many dead or dying slaves thrown into the sea on just such a journey. The number of slaves considered unsaleable in the West Indies or America increased rapidly as they neared their destination, for conditions on board the slave ships deteriorated even further as the voyage progressed. The merchants often collected more money through insurance for 'lost' slaves than by selling them in Virginia.

When we were back at home in England, it occurred to us that we had heard that mournful dirge for a purpose. Perhaps we had a responsibility to pray for those wretched slaves who died uncommitted to the Lord, and to repent of the cruelty of those who were the cause of it. So, in July 1977, with some interested bishops and some members of the Anglican Community of the Resurrection, a Jubilee Eucharist was celebrated at various places throughout England for the specific release of all those who had met their untimely deaths in the Bermuda Triangle. Some months later, in Bermuda itself, the Anglican bishop Anselm Ganders and the Revd Donald Omand, an Anglican priest from Devon, offered the same prayers. The curse of the dreaded place was lifted.

From the time of the Jubilee Eucharist until now – five years – no known, inexplicable accidents have occurred in the Bermuda Triangle. Perhaps evil forces are even now building up again in that place and an accident or disappearance may happen, but we are certain that prayer is the weapon to destroy such evil and to break such a force.

Many authorities are convinced of the possibility of releasing places haunted by the unquiet dead. Donald Omand regularly prays at sites where there have been a number of inexplicable or unusual accidents and invariably the curse of evil is broken. In the course of research into the phenomenon for a documentary report on the subject, a BBC television team investigated the happenings on a stretch of road between Charmouth and Morcombelake in Dorset, on which there were neither dangerous corners nor hidden intersections. Donald Omand had offered prayers at this site and it was found that in the six months prior to his doing so, there had been seventeen accidents on that part of the road. In the subsequent six months, there had not been one single accident.

Sometimes it seems that prayer and an avowed intention to hold a Eucharist in a specific place is sufficient to free that place from being haunted. This was apparent when I was invited to visit a teacher training college in the South of England. The principal asked me to come secretly, as she was having problems with one of the halls of residence in which some students had been refusing to sleep. The building was generally considered to be haunted and every midnight weird noises and screams could be heard in it. According to legend, this had gone on for the past three hundred years, and the principal herself maintained that she had heard strange sounds. She was concerned about their origin and wanted me to offer prayer there in an effort to allay whatever spirit was causing the disturbance.

The fact that this building had the reputation of being haunted had made it something of a tourist attraction in the town and people sometimes came and sat up all through the night in order to listen and watch. This part of the college, situated beside a cathedral, was built on the site of an ancient nunnery so, to emphasize the connection, a group of students had pasted the walls with posters. Some of these depicted religious subjects or were of the cathedral itself but others were of bullfights and other violent secular events. They were all brightly coloured, all of the same size, and all fixed in the same way. Then the students locked and sealed the door to the building. Next morning they found that the religious posters were ripped and lying on the floor while the other posters were still hanging in position on the walls. This happened every time the posters were put up.

Four of us gathered in the building one night, unsure of what to do. We said the Lord's Prayer and asked for guidance. The result was that we decided to form a team of clergy who would come to celebrate the Eucharist there, and three weeks later we assembled secretly for this purpose. However, when we arrived, the principal told us that 'all we needed was a service of praise and thanks to God' because there had been no recurrence of the noises and screams since we had prayed there. We then heard the story that had apparently precipitated our first visit. Some of the more sceptical students had decided to stay through the night in the building, quite sure that nothing unusual would happen. They had been startled to see a figure dressed as a cavalier, complete with the broad-brimmed hat of Charles I's era, emerge through a built-in cupboard door. Then the noise had begun.

They had listened incredulously to the loud screams as the cavalier figure appeared to rape and kill a nun, drop her body down three flights of stairs with a noise like a falling bucket of bricks and then drag it along a corridor to a point where the noise suddenly ceased. The drama was over. However, amid the bedlam the terrified students had knelt by their makeshift beds and prayed.

We retraced the cavalier's route to the place at which the noise had stopped in the middle of the corridor – at that point the floor changed from stone to wooden blocks. Enquiring whether anyone had ever heard of a secret exit from the building, I pulled up a section of the rubber floor-covering. Underneath there was a rusted trapdoor opening onto a flight of steps which, in turn, led down to a cellar. No one present knew that this existed.

I cannot be certain whether a cavalier ever actually raped and killed a nun in that place. I do know for certain that binding all the evil that was manifestly there through the Lord's Prayer and the avowed intention to offer a Eucharist for all needing help and release was sufficient to stop the disturbance of the hauntings permanently.

It is not unusual for people affected by unresolved haunt-ings to be labelled as schizophrenic. Maggie was diagnosed thus and was referred to me by her doctor. She had an invisible friend, Peter, with whom she frequently carried on a conversation. She insisted that he was always trying to help her and other people along the riverbank. I checked her story and discovered that many others had seen the unkempt figure and it was said that he would vanish mysteriously into thin air. He was referred to as Peter the tramp. Perhaps he had been a tramp who had died there on his own and was trying to help others while waiting for help for himself.

Accordingly, three clergymen held a Eucharistic service for Peter right there on the riverbank. During the service, Maggie saw Peter again, this time dressed in white, rising from the river and thanking those who were praying for his release. The clergy themselves felt such a sense of peace that each of them offered to make themselves available to hold such Eucharists in the future and, indeed, have done so many times. Neither Maggie nor anyone else has seen Peter again.

Some years ago, a family with three boys and two girls went to live in a beautiful Tudor-style house in the New Forest. It was built on very old foundations, and a river, complete with two rustic bridges, ran through the garden. There was even a haunted wing. 'No one can sleep there,' they were told. 'It's awful at night.' This was dismissed as so much nonsense by the parents who assumed that bats or owls had been creating a disturbing noise. Indeed, this part of the house was chosen for the children's and visitors' bedrooms.

The family settled in happily, quite discounting tales about the 'hauntings' that they heard from other villagers, from passing gypsies, and even from the postman who would only deliver letters to the box at the gate and refused to come up to the house. Most of the relatives and friends who visited the new house found it a delightful experience and felt a great sense of tranquillity.

However, unaccountable things sometimes happened. Once, a visitor was awakened by a man pulling her arm urgently, another time a nurse heard a voice repeating, 'Please will someone wake up and help me?' Thinking there was someone in distress, she rose and set off down the corridor in the direction of the voice. She was pulled up short when she realized that the voice now came from behind her – she had walked through it! A few months later one of the sons, a stable ten-year-old, cried out in the night as he was awakened by the sliding door of a large wall cupboard in his room being rolled open slowly. One of the daughters was disturbed several times at night by a lot of movement in the corridor outside her room and what she described as 'somebody suffering from flatulence'. Finally, she left out a jar of indigestion tablets with a large notice: 'Next time, try these!'

Sometimes the boys or one of their playmates would demand that 'the old man should be told to go away; he trod on the trains, he's always shuffling about; he doesn't knock anything over and he's very quiet, but he comes through closed doors and windows and appears around corners'. They were matter-of-fact, quite unafraid – it was all just a nuisance. Their father remained sceptical, but one evening, from the boys' bedroom above the room where he sat reading, came a great deal of noise – of clockwork trains, drawers being opened, feet running across the floor and voices. He rushed upstairs. The bedroom was silent and in darkness. The boys were soundly, peacefully asleep, tucked in as usual. He was shaken. As he passed through the hall on his way downstairs, he was further startled by a sudden loud clang on the chandelier – but no one and nothing that he could see had touched it.

At Christmas-time, Elspeth the eldest daughter paid her first visit to the new house. She was a sensible, down-to-earth student who was highly amused by her family's strange tales. She said her prayers and went confidently to bed, happy to be home. At breakfast next morning, she remarked casually, 'I had a long talk with your "friend" in the night. I thought it was you, Daddy, wandering about in the attic looking for something, so I sat up intending to come and help you.' Realizing what she had said, she clapped a hand over her mouth and, with a half-laugh said vehemently, 'It's quite true. He was going up and down in the attic above me but I could see him as well. I don't understand how. He was old and tall, with a moustache and a kind face. He wore a grey suit that was too big and bedroom slippers. He told me his name was Conan Doyle and he called me Elspeth. He said, "I'm sorry I woke you up, I didn't mean to. I am looking for my diary, it's red leather with a black elastic band round it. I hid it somewhere and my wife says it must be found for my memoirs. Please help me. I am so happy that a family of children live here now where my children lived. You lie down and go back to sleep. I promise I won't come again, but if you find my diary please leave it outside the door." Then he was gone.'

Elspeth was unperturbed by the incident but her family were amazed. Her father went to see the parish priest, a man who had lived in the neighbourhood for many years, and discussed the events with him. The priest told him that Conan Doyle had once lived in his house and was buried in the local churchyard. He said, 'I have heard so much about the hauntings at your house – now we know who it is. I think he is ashamed of the diary that he kept for many years. You know, Conan Doyle was once a Christian until he began to dabble in the occult in the name of spiritualism. He died aged seventy – in 1930. I will come to your house and pray so that he may be at peace at last.'

Several members of the family gathered in their music room, part of which had been Conan Doyle's study. The priest prayed an extremely short prayer, unaccompanied by any rites, and committed the troubled author to the Lord. From that day twenty-one years ago, there have been no further manifestations and the house was at rest. Indeed, villagers commented on the new peacefulness which pervaded the whole area, including the country lanes on dark evenings. A newspaper report commented that, a whole week after this prayer of committal, the lift at the doctor's old surgery in Welbeck Street in London had stopped outside his door, regardless of whatever floor button had been pressed. The *Daily Mail* reported that 'Madam Roberts, the famous medium who lives in Kent, had at last received a message from Conan Doyle who wished to apologise for having misled so many people during his lifetime.' His diary has never been found.

Many ghosts are simply the product of overactive imaginations and very often projections of what a person does not want to face. For example, the prudish spinster might see in dark doorways vague figures of men intent upon rape because she fears her sexuality but denies this until it is projected. If she sees ghosts, they too may be like hazy, lustful figures. To her they will be very real and she will share this experience only with those who take her seriously. Regardless of whether or not one believes in objective ghosts, it is necessary to minister to such people and try to help them. One way to do this is to hold a Eucharist for 'whatever may be there', thus allowing the person to forgive the Jungian shadow side they may be projecting and to switch the focus from their own fear to Jesus Christ, thus overcoming that fear. Ghosts may be as subjective and unreal as people in dreams but both reveal a great deal about the parts of the person that need to be touched with the forgiveness and love of Jesus Christ.

I spend less time nowadays in trying to determine whether ghosts are objective or not and more time on uncovering why the living person believes that the dead person, or ghost, needs prayer and reconciliation. As the living person begins to be reconciled with the ghost, that person is at the same time becoming reconciled to the parts of themselves that may be projected into the ghosts. Thus, as the spinster forgives the lustful ghost, she is beginning to be reconciled with her sexual drives and to bring them to Jesus Christ, even though the 'ghosts' may have no objective reality.

We do not know whether these 'haunting' spirits are good or neutral or evil nor do we know what might be the interaction of these three. We cannot be sure of the best way to release homes, roads, classrooms or battlefields and we cannot tell whether evil builds up again in places that have been released; if it does, how could it be prevented? We do know with absolute certainty that places and people are freed as we bind any evil spirits, offer the Eucharist for whichever dead person may need release, and commit ourselves to Jesus Christ, the Lord over all powers (Rom. 8.38–39).

Dom Robert Petitpierre, a Benedictine monk and exorcist of places, uses four traditional steps. First, a general exorcism of all the rooms in a house, using holy water; second, a celebration of the Eucharist with prayers for the dead; third, a blessing of the whole building and of each room; fourth, another celebration of the Eucharist in honour of the patron, or of St Michael and All Angels, concluding with the praise of the Te Deum or Gloria. The house is then under the Lord's protection.

Although England may house half of the world's ghosts at the present time, the belief that places may need to be released and protected is very primitive. There is a long tradition of pilgrimage to sacred places in all religions.

For nearly two thousand years Christians have journeyed to the Holy Land to follow reverently in Jesus Christ's steps. The Christian Bible also records the desecration of places as by the blood of Cain (Gen. 4.10). Jesus often passed by the Jerusalem garbage dump, Gehenna in the valley of Hinnom, which had been desecrated by pagan sacrifices of children. This place could make a Jew 'unclean'. The evil there was acknowledged by everyone and became an image for hell (Matt. 5.22). Similarly, in mediaeval times, places desecrated by a black mass were 'unclean' until they had been purified by blessing.

Farmers today often continue the old custom of blessing their fields on rogation days; ships and buildings may be blessed when they are built; churches are always consecrated when they are erected. 'O Father, deign these walls to bless; Fill with thy love their emptiness' (Whittier). Many such traditions have been lost, however, because the spirit world in which mediaeval people believed is generally derided as superstition. Thus, people tend to be insensitive to the ability of some places (for example,

Lourdes) to open them to receive Christ's spirit while other places can open them to the spirits of the dead or of the evil one.

Sometimes, places need to be released not only from the dead but also from occult movement. A doctor friend maintained that he frequently heard and saw a black dog bounding up and down the stairs in three jumps at night. Although his wife did not believe him, I did. So we bound the evil, commanding it to leave and prayed for whomsoever might need prayer. The dog ceased its nightly romping. A year later, when the doctor was removing a radiator which had been set into a wall, he discovered behind it a black dog painted on the wall together with bits of candle-grease, clearly the remnants of some occult ceremony of long ago. His wife was then quite convinced that the doctor had not been imagining things!

This is not an isolated case. Dr Kurt Koch agrees that hauntings commonly occur where there have been occult practices. He writes: 'One of the most puzzling manifestations is that of spook phenomena at the scene of action or the homes of occultists, not only while they are still alive but even after death. As long as the occult practitioner is alive, the spook phenomena can be understood by Bender's theory of the separated existence of dissociated psychic powers. The persistence of the phenomena after the practitioner's death, however, is beyond rational explanation. Here we must resort to a transcendental explanation, unless scientific psychical research should one day supply the key to the mystery.'[1]

Indeed, until we have a better scientific explanation, we should use whatever means we have to bring peace to a disturbed place. Firstly, to renounce any and all occult involvement and bind the evil one, commanding it to leave, and remembering to dispose of spiritualist and occult objects that attract spirits to places. Secondly, to discover if possible the identity of the person who may be 'haunting' and release him or her through prayer, the Eucharist being especially effective. If the identity cannot be established, then the prayers should be for whomsoever might need prayer, including those hurt by the dead person. Thirdly, to require everyone present to commit themselves to the Lord and the protection of his angels, so that his presence can fill the whole place and there is no room for evil.

7

The Dark World

In 1964, Bishop Mortimer, then Bishop of Exeter, invited me to join the newly-formed Exeter Exorcism Commission. Although I had been in private psychiatric practice for only a year, I had twelve cases to present to the Commission because a number of doctors had referred to me patients who had been damaged by the occult.

The Commission's work grew from that first meeting, when only two Anglican bishops answered the invitation, to the present time when thirty-eight bishops are represented. Nowadays, every diocese in England has an appointed exorcist. The church is beginning to realize the dangers of the occult. But I do not want to exaggerate the prevalence of demonic involvement as this accounted for only 4 per cent of the cases which I treated in hospital and outpatients clinics. The percentage of such cases now referred to me is rising, however, and my patients tend to be those who have failed to respond to other medical and psychiatric treatment. Many people, untouched by years of such treatment, have been cured by prayer, even when they had no knowledge that prayer was being offered on their behalf.

When there is a suspicion that occult forces are at work in a person's life, a prerequisite of any subsequent treatment is a thorough medical examination. Someone suspected of being under demonic control may in fact be suffering from depressive psychosis, schizophrenia or the effects of other organic psychoses. The person could be acutely neurotic, hidden aspects of his personality or an upsurge image from his deep unconscious could be the cause. Although all such diagnoses should be treated as psychiatric disorders, they do not exclude demonic control.

There may be illness that is solely mental; there may be mental illness together with demonic control; there may be demonic control alone. The test for this is not the presence or absence of mental illness but rather whether there is a response to prayer and to the Eucharist. This diagnosis should be as accurate as possible.

Muriel, a woman in her thirties, claimed that she was 'possessed' and that she saw devils dancing in front of her. Her Roman Catholic priest sent her to me for a psychiatric opinion hoping that, if her story were true, I might be able to identify the 'devils' so that they could be exorcized. Muriel certainly seemed depressed and confused. She was also very pale. She described her 'devils' as little black things that danced in front of her eyes whenever she rose suddenly from her bed or from an armchair. A simple blood count revealed a marked degree of anaemia and she also had very low blood pressure. Nevertheless I had a clear conviction, which had come during my early morning time of quiet prayer, that part of her problem was connected with a walking stick of some kind.

At her next visit I gave Muriel a prescription for anaemia and, as she was about to leave, asked her about the walking stick. She blushed and muttered, 'What do you mean?' I said that I did not know exactly what I meant and asked her again about the stick. Finally, she told me about a jewel-encrusted crozier which had been stolen by one of her ancestors. It had lain hidden under the floorboards in her family home for several generations. After some research, she was helped to arrange for the valuable crozier to be restored to the descendants of its rightful owner. Within two weeks Muriel was transformed – a free and happy woman.

I now concentrate less on patients 'possessed', like Muriel, who mainly require medication, and more on patients who are truly in bondage through the occult. This means all the practices which seek power or knowledge from a source contrary to God's teachings (Deut. 5.6–10; 18.10–12). For instance, astrology, ouija boards, automatic writing, horoscopes, fortune telling, divination, seances, tarot cards, witchcraft and transcendental meditation[1] are all tools of the evil one. They may be practised innocently at first and just for fun, but they lead away from God. Psychiatry acknowledges the reality that the occult opens the door to the evil spirit world. Psychiatric researchers are even documenting cures, such as a change in sexual orientation, brought about through exorcism prayer and bringing freedom and escape from that world. In an article in the British medical journal *The Practitioner* (March 1974) Dr Richard Mackarness (Assistant Psychiatrist at Park Prewett Hospital, Basingstoke in Hampshire) recorded how exorcism helped a patient suffering from a schizoid illness.

'Over the past ten years in this country there has been an explosion of interest in the occult, particularly among the young. This increased interest has coincided with increased abuse of "soft" and "hard" drugs and the two things may well be connected. Inevitably, just as psychiatrists are seeing more patients for drug abuse, so a number of patients involved with occult practices are coming into mental hospitals. Some of these latter are severely disturbed and do not respond well to orthodox psychiatric treatment with electro-convulsive therapy and psychotropic drugs. In some cases, only exorcism and prayer will help them.'

After trying the usual drugs for such patients, with negative results, Dr Mackarness concluded: 'Having come to the end of orthodox therapeutic resources, I began to suspect that I was dealing with a case of the possession syndrome. A colleague, Dr Kenneth McAll, had recently published an article on this subject so I decided to call him in to see the patient and discuss exorcism. I brought a crucifix from home and, together with a nurse he brought with him to act as a chaperone, we performed the service. The result was dramatic. The patient said she felt better at once and thereafter made an uninterrupted recovery. Her drugs were quickly tapered off and have not been resumed.'

The patient Dr Mackarness was treating was a thirty-eight-year-old woman factory worker hospitalized as 'schizophrenic'. She was answering imaginary telephone calls from her dead father and could 'see footsteps' across the ward floor. Her insight was poor, she was confused in thought and limited in speech by a low IQ. There was nothing physically wrong with her except that she sometimes slept badly. She was a small, anxious, self-conscious woman who had no previous family history of mental disturbance.

When I was called to give a second psychiatric opinion, this woman told me that five months earlier she had visited a spiritualist couple for healing. She had asked them for help because she thought that she 'must be a drug addict' despite the fact that she was taking only a mild tranquillizer. The couple had passed their hands around her and she had become very frightened and hastily returned home. Then she began to have hallucinations, imagining the healer 'in her house and garden' and hearing his voice on the telephone. Sleepless and disturbed, she had been admitted to hospital.

It seemed possible that the cause of her trouble might be an occult force and so we decided to pray while the patient was in her deluded state. We prayed very simply to God for guidance and protection, in Jesus Christ's name, said the Lord's Prayer and commanded any evil to leave peacefully. No further treatment was necessary. The patient was healed from that moment and returned home two days later to her husband and teenage son. Five years later the woman had no memory of this occasion.[2]

I learned from the staff that there were other patients in the same hospital as a result of this spiritualist's activity. I visited him and he confessed that he had caused other disasters. He decided not to interfere with people again, but to learn about the life of Jesus Christ from the Bible, a book he had never dared to read.

It is not unusual for those needing deliverance from the evil one to react against sacred things and prayer. Even the offering of silent prayers (which eliminates the possibility of suggestion) can disturb them, and their erratic behaviour can be turned on and off simply by starting and stopping a silent prayer. This can help considerably in making a diagnosis.

A girl of eighteen went to see a film about the devil and the occult. Badly shaken by what she saw, she realized that such memories usually fade with time. In her case, however, she became increasingly haunted by visions of the devil and voices which told her to destroy herself. She had to stop work and started to take drugs to which she gradually became addicted. Nine months later she came to consult me, blaming herself for going to see the film in the first place. It was obvious that to give her tranquillizers would have been of no more use than putting a poultice on a broken leg, so I suggested that we should pray together. The girl readily agreed. Very simply, I prayed in the name of Jesus Christ that this evil power would lose its control over her life. From that moment she had no more visions, heard no more voices and stopped taking drugs.

The Medical Officer of a Bible Training College referred Brian to me. He was a divorced student in his late twenties whose behaviour was disrupting the life of the College. He could not sleep and was full of inexplicable terrors.

Brian told me that throughout his childhood his parents had quarrelled continually, had finally divorced, and that he had left home as soon as possible to join the Royal Air Force. Friends he had made there introduced him to the ouija board, numerology and tarot cards. He became involved with astrology and joined a witches' coven but was extremely alarmed when, having learned to use 'automatic writing', he found that he repeatedly and uncontrollably spelled out the words 'German murder'.

On consulting a female medium – who made use of family photographs in order to receive messages from the dead – Brian was told that he resembled very closely a great uncle who had been killed in the war. The woman at one time had been a keen worker in a nonconformist church but, after discovering her 'powers', the very mention of

Jesus Christ's name was sufficient to prevent her from functioning as a medium.

Brian developed a strong desire to find a personal Christian faith and, eventually, had applied for training at the College. He could not forget his past involvements, however, and was increasingly haunted by the same words. When we drew up his Family Tree we found that the great uncle of whom the medium had spoken had been blown up by a German landmine during the war and had never been properly committed to the Lord. We held a service for him and Brian asked forgiveness for all his evil, occult behaviour. He knew both forgiveness and release and he completed his training without difficulty.

Forgiveness and renunciation

It is not necessary to be involved directly in the occult to receive occult damage. Through their own occult involvement parents can even harm their children. John was four years old and was having increasingly frequent epileptiform attacks during which it took three adults to restrain him. All breakable objects in his home had to be kept out of the way and he could never be left alone in case he had an attack. When I visited him we spent a pleasant, perfectly quiet time together, playing with trains. Finally, I gave up trying to learn anything from John and went to talk with his father.

As we locked ourselves in his study to avoid being interrupted by the child, I prayed silently for some clue to the situation. I was surprised to see a quantity of spiritualist literature on the shelves and the man astonished me by telling me that he had been experimenting with 'radionics' and that a spiritualist medium had been his 'great friend' for the past fifteen years. Immediately and without thought

I pronounced, 'When you seek forgiveness from God and burn these books, your son will be free! You, a Methodist minister, are breaking God's laws.' The man reacted furiously and ordered me out of the house without further discussion.

A little while later, John began to have an attack which lasted, intermittently, for thirty-six hours. His parents and the friends who were helping were all exhausted but not the child.

In desperation his father sought the help of a neighbouring Anglican vicar. Together they went to the parish church and, at the altar, the father asked for God's forgiveness for the harm he had caused through his dabbling in the occult. Afterwards, he burned all of his books on the occult and felt cleansed. John has never had another 'attack' since. His teacher at the little school for maladjusted children which he attended was amazed at the change in him. He is now at a normal school and doing well. And his father now regularly conducts healing services in his own church.

It may seem unfair that a child should suffer the effects of a father's occult involvement but the evil one will cause suffering and distress to any who may have inherited such an interest, albeit unknowingly. God commands us not to worship any idols. He says: 'I, the Lord your God, am a jealous God, punishing the children for the sin of the fathers to the third and fourth generation of those who hate me' (Exod. 20.5).

Thus, some ministers of deliverance, such as the Revd Pat Brooks, even demand that the 'possessed' person renounces a list of occult offences which his ancestors may have committed. 'If they will confess their sins and the sins of their fathers . . .' (Lev. 26.40). He says: 'Since an important part of successful ministry appears to be breaking the demonic heredity in the family line, we all repeat aloud the entire list of offences. After this confession comes the renunciation: "I now break, in the name of Jesus Christ, all psychic heredity, and any demonic hold upon my family line as a result of the disobedience of any of my ancestors."'³

The same emphasis on renunciation of inherited bondage comes from Dr Kurt Koch whose affirmation for those in bondage is: 'In the name of Jesus Christ I renounce all the works of the devil together with the occult practices of my forefathers, and I subscribe myself to Jesus Christ, my Lord and Saviour, both now and for ever.'⁴ Dr Koch uses this formula because he has dealt with over ten thousand cases of occult bondage and has often traced patterns of inherited disasters through several generations. He writes:

'In the families of "charmers" whose history I could trace for three or four generations, we find effects such as death in a mental home, melancholia, suicide, and fatal accidents as a constantly recurring and therefore normal pattern ... Symptoms of this kind which occur in well-nigh every family of "charmers" always alerts me to occult involvement.'⁵

Dr Koch also recommends release through the processes which I use, that is, accurate diagnosis, renunciation, confession of sin and its absolution, prayer of command and, importantly, the building up of life with the help of a loving community involved with God's word, prayer and especially, the Eucharist. Often the Lord shortens this process. In the case of the schizophrenic patient of Dr Mackarness, the deliverance prayer was prayed immediately. Frequently, the deliverance prayer has to be deferred until the person can ask for forgiveness and renounce his voluntary involvement in the occult, as in the case of John's father.

Prayer for deliverance[6]

Unlike both of these situations in which the people concerned were present, deliverance can occur by praying at a distance. Such prayer is especially helpful when the person needing deliverance refuses help, or is not free enough to renounce occult involvement fully, or is the victim of involuntary involvement.

A wealthy, married woman of forty-five was sent to me by her psychiatrist. She had been an alcoholic for several years but, strangely, when she was staying in our home she was perfectly normal and apparently had no inclination to drink, whereas in her own home her constant drinking disrupted her family's life. The woman's mother was deeply involved in spiritualism and was in the process of making spiritualistic contact with her dead husband. From my questioning of this woman I gathered that her excessive drinking was connected with her mother's curse upon her for refusing to sign some legal documents without being able to read them first.

A group of us decided that, without the family's knowledge, we would arrange for prayers to be said every Thursday afternoon mainly by clergymen, in different parts of the country. We broke the curse on this alcoholic woman and put the protection of the Lord's grace and angels around her. Even though the patient did not know about our prayer circle, she stopped drinking on the first Thursday without any warning and, a few weeks later, she and her family celebrated their first alcohol-free Christmas for many years. Her delighted husband began to attend church regularly and eventually became a churchwarden. Even the stormy marriages of the couple's two sons were reconciled during the following few months.

Building up life

However effective prayer for deliverance is, it can be blocked later if the person does not use the resulting freedom to make Satan leave and to ask Christ to take over. One lady who engaged in a lesbian relationship entertained herself by inviting people, including myself, to pray for her deliverance. Afterwards, however, she continued in her same way of life, and did not use her freedom to choose to commit herself to the Lord Jesus Christ. I refused to continue to visit her and told her that I would return only if she really wanted to straighten out her life. If the freedom after a deliverance prayer is used to allow the evil one to stay (through patterns of sin, resentment or continuing occult involvement), that freedom is usually soon lost.

Conversely, if a person uses that freedom to invite Jesus Christ to be the centre of his/her life, the evil one cannot remain. Because it is vitally important to build up spiritual resources, occasionally we have taken into our home people needing deliverance just so that they can be provided with a loving Christian community. As they are loved by us and the Lord, they receive, also, an inner healing of past traumatic relationships or events. If they had been hurt by a father, for instance, they would grow in knowing God as Father so that the hurt invited God rather than the evil one.

Unless a wound is healed by counselling, fellowship and prayer, it becomes an open door for the return of the evil one. To help people to close such subconscious doors to anyone but the Lord, we also teach them how to listen with a clear mind in their waking thoughts. In this way, they soon experience guidance from God. The more a person can focus on a committed relationship with Jesus Christ, the easier it is to deliver that person for ever from the control of the evil one. There would be less shame over requiring deliverance prayer if people understood that deliverance occurs more because they are truly repentant and full of Jesus' power and forgiveness so that evil cannot stay, than because they are so full of evil.

For twenty years doctors had tried to treat a forty-one-year-old engineer who suffered from gastric pain and tension. In addition, he had recently complained of a 'tight band' around his head, had become increasingly depressed and was unable to work. Investigation by hospital specialists had all proved negative, and he failed to respond to any treatment. He could not sleep and his appetite deteriorated in spite of increased drug dosage, until finally he contemplated suicide. Then he was referred to me.

He appeared to be suffering from a self-induced depression with the typical pattern of early morning wakening. He remembered his dreams and these were mainly concerned with disturbing conversations with dead friends. I questioned him carefully about his beliefs and religious attitudes. He and his family had been Anglicans originally but, in recent years, had come to know a woman who advertised herself as a psychologist. In fact, she was a crystal gazer and the man and his family came to rely more and more on her advice.

After making some slight alterations in his medication and adding a course of vitamins, I introduced him to the idea of special prayer.[7] This laid particular emphasis on writing down any thoughts which came during the early morning period of private contemplation. Ten days later, he brought me a list of these thoughts, all of which were highly relevant and practical. One suggestion was that his headaches were largely due to lack of fresh air and exercise; another, that during the week he should go to a Eucharist and become involved in his local church. He also realized that he should be aware of the evil which was controlling him through the association with the crystal gazer, and that he should perform his own renunciation and deliverance.

This he did by simply holding the Bible and saying firmly, 'Satan, get out!' The change in him was marked and rapid. He became peaceful and relaxed and began sleeping normally. His energy returned and now, four years later, he has established for himself an international reputation in his particular engineering field.

Although his wife was delighted that her husband had recovered, she did not entirely agree with his new thinking about Jesus Christ. She had been considered 'the pillar of the household and was always right'. On her own initiative, she went again to consult the crystal gazer. When she returned home, she was disorientated, noisy and distressed, with paranoid ideas that her neighbours were trying to harass her.

Her own doctor was called and he arranged for her immediate admission to hospital. While we were all waiting in the same room, her husband and I said the prayers of exorcism but she did not appear to derive any benefit from them.

Next morning when she awoke in hospital she felt well and acted quite normally. After a couple of days she was sent home and has had no further trouble; no one in the family has consulted the crystal gazer again.

This husband had achieved personal deliverance by his own efforts but the care of a Christian community is essential for more severe cases of long-term control, in order that the one who has been delivered may form new habits.

An unusual and extreme example of this occurred in a lady in her mid-sixties who came from Australia. For fifty years she had constantly heard 'voices' with whom she conversed, calling them by name, and in all those years no medical treatment had helped her. Frequently, the advice of her 'voices' was disastrous but she could not escape their influence. They called themselves 'The Three Beasties' and had taken over when, as a non-Christian of sixteen years old, she had been anaesthetised for an appendix operation. Since there is more prayer power and discernment when praying with a team, four of us joined together to pray for her deliverance and freedom. We seemed to be successful for the 'voices', which had plagued her for fifty years, ceased.

However, that same evening, she discovered to her dismay that she had no will of her own after being totally controlled for so long. She did not know how to use a fork or even how to wash. It was only after nine months of patient training in the formation of new habit patterns and confidence-building that she was able to fly back to Australia by herself.

I cannot usually offer such intensive follow-up care to my patients, so I often ask that a person seeking deliverance prayer is accompanied by a friend who will continue such follow-up if necessary. Deliverance is not a one-step cure but brings with it new freedom to choose new ways. The crutch of 'the devil made me do it' must be abandoned and replaced with insight and understanding of what prevents new ways not being freely chosen. Long-term bad habits must still be struggled with and overcome while new, good habits are being formed. It is easier to remove evil spirits by deliverance than to keep them out by leading a well-balanced life involving prayer and the Eucharist to build up Christ's influence.

It is extremely important to follow-up a deliverance with a focus on the power of Jesus Christ rather than on the presence of demons. Very often it is followed by a period of temptation where the evil one tries to return by making the freed person doubt his/her new freedom. They may awaken in the middle of the night and feel again an evil presence, or experience the same evil compulsion and think it is demonic. They must learn to look upon it merely as a bad habit pattern that they can now freely change with the continuing help of Christian discipline.

When these times of temptation come, the person must focus on the power of Jesus Christ and calmly assert it, knowing that the evil one has no more rights unless doubts or repeated sin invite him back. 'If the Son sets you free, you will be free indeed' (John 8.36). When a patient consults me about a recurring attack after being freed, I usually recommend that he prays the Lord's Prayer and visualizes the Father sending his angels to protect him. If this is done with conviction, usually no more is needed, especially when the patient removes himself from a bad environment to a loving Christian community and continues to be filled with Jesus' protective life promised by him at the Eucharist. If the attacks continue, then I must discover why the patient cannot let go of the evil one, and try to perform further inner healing of the traumas that are blocking development of the total relationship with Jesus.

Ruth was an intelligent woman, though very thin and fearful. She came to see me with her husband because of her frequent outbursts of violent temper which, so far as she was concerned, were associated with acute pain. Between 1946 and 1972 she had undergone numerous investigations in hospital and several exploratory operations. Nothing had helped her.

I gave her a routine physical examination but could find only one abnormality – her right kidney seemed to move around in the abdomen. When I mentioned this to the couple later, Ruth's husband became very angry indeed. He insisted that everything possible had been done medically and that they had consulted me because I was a psychiatrist, so would I please mind my own business! Without further discussion, he took his wife by the arm and stormed out of the house.

Astonished by this extraordinary attitude, I was almost equally surprised when Ruth returned alone to see me a few months later. She had made no progress. I sent her to the X-ray department of the local hospital for an investigation of her kidney's apparent mobility but neither they, nor Ruth herself, seemed to have heard of a floating kidney. In desperation, I sought the help of a private radiologist who carried out the necessary tests. The X-rays confirmed the suspicion that the kidney moved about 6 cm between the standing and lying down positions, a clear indication that an operation was essential.

Two surgeons refused to perform it and the third reluctantly agreed only when I offered to assist him, having done three similar operations myself some years previously. Ruth's operation revealed that, in fact, her kidney was able to move both vertically and laterally, but a simple matter of stitching secured it in its correct position. I assumed that, having successfully cured her physical pain, the problem of her violent outbursts of temper remained to be dealt with but, from the day of her operation, there was no further display of temper and Ruth, after twenty-six years, became a normal, controlled woman. She had not needed deliverance prayer; she had not needed repentance; she *had* needed to have a straightforward kidney operation!

Because it is vitally important for the delivered person to receive Christ's life into his emptiness, I now prefer to take a deliverance through the Eucharist whenever possible.[8] If a person experiences his new freedom through this rather than through private deliverance prayers, he is more likely to continue to take the Eucharist regularly and will focus more on a relationship with Jesus than with me. Since the evil spirits fear this power, they often try to prevent a freed person from taking the Eucharist. (Indeed, witches acknowledge that their chief enemy is the forgiving power of the Eucharist, so their ultimate desecration is a black mass.)

The Eucharist can free even the most difficult cases; those most deeply involved in the occult. Friends brought a nineteen-year-old girl to me who suffered from hallucinations. She was notorious for her performances of the black arts which she had learned from her grandmother before her death. The girl was persuaded to burn all her occult books and she then attended an evangelical service of the Lord's Supper for her own cleansing. In the same service her grandmother was recommitted to the Lord. Next morning the girl felt totally free of any hallucinations and very happy.

On the following Sunday, she stood up in church and told the whole congregation about her new-found freedom. Whether the service is called the Eucharist of the Resurrection, the Eucharist for the deceased, the Lord's Supper, the Breaking of Bread, Holy Communion or the Requiem Mass does not matter. The overwhelming effect of the power that is generated is all-embracing.

Although at a Eucharist service of deliverance I may bind whatever behaviour (anxiety, fatigue, depression, etc.) may be preventing a person from fully participating in the Eucharist, there have been occasions when an ordinary, straightforward Eucharist with no extra prayers was all that was necessary to free those in the evil one's control.

Nancy, a teenager who lived in Hampshire, suffered from agoraphobia. The very thought of going out anywhere would make her sick. Thus she would develop stomach upsets and was unable to go to school. Nancy's frightening abnormality, however, was that she constantly saw her dead grandfather walking around upstairs in her home, waving out of the window and winking at her from his photograph on the wall. Her grandmother and the two aunts with whom she lived claimed that they also saw him. One of her aunts told me that Nancy would sit as if in a trance, rapidly drawing straight lines across a sheet of paper. When they were examined through a magnifying glass, the lines were revealed as words. They were 'conversations' she was holding with her grandfather.

An exorcist who was consulted reported that this was automatic writing and Nancy was under the influence of devil possession. The local vicar was asked to hold a Eucharistic service in Nancy's home. I expected him to say a prayer of deliverance for Nancy and recommittal prayers for her grandfather. He duly celebrated the Eucharist but omitted to pray either before or during the service for these two specific intentions.

I was rather annoyed but the Eucharist alone was sufficient to dispel the troublesome ancestor for ever. He did not appear again to Nancy and their written 'conversations' ceased. The girl's agoraphobia was immediately overcome and she changed so much that her two aunts were converted to Christ.

The Lord seems to use our fumblings and mistakes and even our good intentions to free people; he wants us to trust in him rather than insist on presenting a perfectly performed ritual to him. I was too much concerned with whether we were praying for an ancestor, that is grandfather, or for general freedom from evil spirits through the deliverance prayer of command. When ancestors were present, I thought that they were causing the suffering in order to attract the attention of the living so that they could be released.

Sometimes, however, as I confront the evil one it seems to me possible that the suffering of the living is, in fact, the work of the evil one. The evil one can try to torture us with physical and mental illnesses which leave us emotionally focused only on ourselves so that we forget to reach out to help the dead. Evil symptoms and their inevitable fruit of despair which leads to suicide, bear the marks of the evil one battling with those who are sensitive to the uncommitted dead. Perhaps this is an act from the great drama described in the Bible: 'For our struggle is not against flesh and blood, but against the rulers, against the authorities, against the powers of this dark world and against the spiritual forces of evil in the heavenly realms' (Eph. 6.12).

As we learn more of the mystery of the collective unconscious with its realm of archetypes and spirits, we shall understand precisely who is hurting the living. Until that time, we must continue to pray that both the dead and the living may be filled with Jesus' love and, through the Eucharist, we can destroy whatever invites evil spirits. In Nancy's case, through the automatic writing of letters to her dead grandfather, evil spirits were able to take control until, at the Eucharist, Jesus filled the loneliness in both Nancy and her grandfather so that the evil spirits had to leave, even without a command. The evil one cannot stay in a relationship which is being filled by Jesus Christ.

8

'To the Lord in prayer'

My God is a God of love. I have the right, bought by Jesus
Christ and given freely to me, to bring to him in prayer
anyone, living or dead, any situation or any circumstance
that I choose. My faith assures me and my experience
convinces me that his healing can be effective beyond 'all
that I can ask or desire'. I do not and cannot understand
how this happens but this in no way alters the fact that
it does happen. Our Christian ministry does not rest
upon our interpretation of what happens, but upon the
evident healing results.

At one stage of my Christian life I felt that we could not
pray for the dead since judgement came immediately after
death. 'Just as man is destined to die once, and after that
to face judgment, so Christ was sacrificed once to take
away the sins of many people; and He will appear a second
time . . .' (Heb. 9.27). These words do not specify when
judgement will occur – it could be taken as happening
parallel to the second coming of Christ. The Old Testament
prohibits consulting the dead and being led by them as in
spiritualism (Deut. 18.11), but does not prohibit praying
for the dead. The New Testament is largely as silent on
this question as on the first thirty years of Jesus' life or on
how his earthly parents Joseph and Mary were laid to rest
and mourned. (The apostle John concludes that there are

still many other parts of Jesus' life that are not recorded
(John 21.25).)

Our loving God wants to save us so much that he sent
his Son to die for us in propitiation of our sins and he
tells us that not even death can separate us from his love
(Rom. 8.38, 39). Even if we turn our back on him, his love
and mercy towards us endure for ever (1 Cor. 13). We can
help one another because through baptism we are all
members of Christ's body. Our baptism is so powerful
that it wipes away distinctions between Jew and Greek,
male and female, servant and master until we are all equal
before Christ. The early Christians realized that this unity
lasted beyond death and bound the living and the dead
into the 'communion of saints'. Since both the living and
the dead are members of Christ's body (1 Cor. 15.29), we
can ask Christ to help the dead to receive his love and
forgiveness as he offers it through the Eucharist.

Precisely how Jesus touches the dead we bring to him
is a mystery we shall understand only when we are with
him in heaven. We know that as we pray for the dead and
they surrender their lives to Jesus Christ, and to living out
his will, people are healed. There is a choice between being
like the Pharisees who doubted until they could explain
everything logically, or walking in faith as the blind man
who, although he did not fully understand, nevertheless
averred, 'One thing I do know; I was blind but now
I see' (John 9.25). There is a long Christian tradition of
praying for the dead. The importance of loving and forgiving the dead through prayer is taught by many of the
early fathers such as Tertullian, Origen, Ephraem, Cyprian,
Ambrose, Augustine, Basil, Gregory of Nyssa, Gregory
of Nazianzus, Gregory the Great and Martin Luther.[1]
The stress they place on asking for the dead to receive

forgiveness and risen life echoes the attitude of the Jews in the second century BC who praised Judas Maccabeus for praying for his dead soldiers 'to be freed from sin' with 'the resurrection of the dead in view'.

'He [Judas Maccabeus] then took up a collection among all his soldiers amounting to 2,000 silver drachmas which he sent to Jerusalem to provide for an expiatory sacrifice. In doing this he acted in a very excellent and noble way; inasmuch as he had the resurrection of the dead in view. For if he were not expecting the fallen to rise again, it would have been useless and foolish to pray for them in death. But if he did this with a view to the splendid reward that awaits those who had gone to rest in Godliness, it was a Holy and pious thought. Thus he made atonement for the dead that they might be freed from this sin' (2 Macc. 12.42–46).

The promptness in praying for the sinful soldiers, a generous collection donated by the whole army, and the presumption that the priests in Jerusalem would accept this collection indicate that this was no innovation but was an accepted part of Jewish religious life at that time.

The translations of the Bible which follow the Hebrew rather than the Greek Old Testament (Septuagint) do not always contain this passage about Judas Maccabeus. The early church of St Paul, however, was a Greek-speaking church, which believed that the Septuagint, with this passage, was the word of God. St Paul's Corinthian church followed a mysterious practice of using the prayers of baptism to help the dead (1 Cor. 15.29) which the saint does not condemn as heresy, even in this letter in which he is prepared to condemn so many things. He mentions almost casually, and thus gives tacit approval to, the Corinthian church's practice of drawing the dead into the light of Christ through prayer. St Paul (or the author of 2 Tim. 1.18) even prays for the dead Onesiphorus to find mercy.

One of the most obvious indications that praying for the dead is acceptable comes from Daniel, who asked for God's forgiveness for present sin and for the sin of his forebears: '... I was ... praying, confessing my sin and the sin of my people Israel ...' (Dan. 9.20). The Lord was so pleased with Daniel's prayer that he sent Gabriel with an answer of forgiveness for the present and past sins that had been confessed: 'Seventy "sevens" are decreed for your people and your holy city to finish transgression, to put an end to sin, to atone for wickedness ...' (Dan. 9.24).

In the same tradition as Daniel, Baruch also prays that Yahweh should forgive and 'remember not the misdeeds of our fathers' (Baruch 3.1–8). Thus, in the Old Testament there was a specific awareness that in prayer we can ask and receive the Lord's forgiveness for the dead. The apparent injustice of 'the sins of the fathers' being punished until the third and fourth generation is reconciled when it is understood that God is, in fact, encouraging the living to help their sinful fathers, through prayer, by asking him for forgiveness on their behalf.

The New Testament, written by early Christians, was the basis of teaching for those who followed the apostles. We know that those who were closest in time to the events of the New Testament, prayed for their dead. During persecution they hid in the catacombs where they buried their dead and carved on their tombs requests for prayer. For example, on one catacomb tombstone (now in the Lateran Museum at Rome) the husband declared that he set the inscription for his beloved wife Lucifera 'in order that all brethren who read it may pray for her, that she may reach God'.

Other second and third century inscriptions ask for peace and refreshment or for admission among the saints. One authority describes how the accompanying pictures relate to the same theme: 'The faithfull prayed for the dead, entreating God to protect their souls, as He protected Daniel in the lions' den, the three young men in the furnace, Noah in the ark, and Susannah against the two Elders. With the same intention and in order to invite the visitors to these subterranean cemeteries to pray for the dead, these biblical figures were depicted near sepulchres – Daniel and Noah in the hypogeum of the Flavii as early as the first century, and all four together at the beginning of the second century in the Capella Greca.'[2]

Thus, Christians 'as early as the first century' were aware that it was incumbent upon them not to abandon their dead but to continue to help them towards God. They offered the Eucharist on the tombs of their martyrs and on anniversaries prayed for the 'lesser dead' entombed around them. In the East John Chrysostom,[3] and in the West Cyprian (AD 245), each regarded this practice as emanating from the apostles' teachings.

Jungmann in *Mass of the Roman Rite*[4] traces the development of the offering of this memorial Eucharist and asserts that its roots are as ancient as the pre-Christian graveside memorial meal (*refrigerium*) and sacrifices. Early Eucharists, such as that reported in the Apocryphal Acts of St John (AD 170) were often conducted at the grave either on the third day after burial or a year later, as occurred with the annual memorial mass in Smyrna for Polycarp (AD 155). By the third century, it was customary to pray for the dead on their memorial day.

Tertullian writes: 'The faithful wife would pray for the soul of her deceased husband, particularly on the anniversary of his falling asleep. And if she fails to do so, she has repudiated her husband as far as in her lies.'[5] Tertullian advises a widower not to marry again because he would find himself in the embarrassing position of still praying for his first wife.

The offering of such prayers was not only a private, individual practice. In AD 337, the Emperor Constantine died and his body was placed before the altar while priests and people prayed for his soul.[6] Also by the fourth century, several commemorative Eucharists were held, especially on the third, seventh, ninth, thirtieth and fortieth days after a person's death; two hundred years later, priests were saying the Eucharist for the dead not just on the third day but on a series of consecutive days ranging from three to forty days. Unfortunately, this holy rite deteriorated by the Middle Ages into a magical mumbo-jumbo which promised unfailing results from the repetition of a set number of hurried masses. The reformers rightly rejected this abuse but, in rejecting the 'magic', they rejected a deep Christian tradition.

Jungmann[7] also traces the history of the Eucharistic texts that reflect the early Christian concern with praying for the dead. The *Canon of Hippolytus* (33:1.169), probably reflecting third-century practice, specifically mentions praying for the dead. The *Apostolic Constitution* contains the formulary, 'Let us pray for our brethren who sleep in Christ; that God, who in His love for men has received the love of the departed one, may forgive him every fault, and in mercy and clemency receive him into the bosom of Abraham with those who in this life have pleased God.'[8] In the fifth century, Christians remembered the dead at the Kyrie (Lord, have mercy) especially on weekdays. Thus, the earliest daily Bobbio Missal (AD 700) used in Irish monasteries has a special prayer for the dead. This continues in the Roman rite. In late eighth-century times, during the Eucharistic prayer, the Canon read from diptychs (that is, hinged two-leaved writing tablets) the names of prominent deceased civil and church authorities so that everyone could pray for them.

A strong tradition of offering prayers for the dead also exists outside the Roman rite. John Chrysostom stated, 'When that awe-inspiring sacrifice lies displayed on the altar, how shall we not prevail with God by our entreaties for the dead?'[9] Egypt's oldest formulary, the Serapion, has a prayer for the deceased: 'Sanctify all who have died in the Lord and number them among your holy troops and give them peace and dwelling in thy kingdom.' Thus, both Eastern and Western Christians have prayed for their dead throughout centuries and continue to do so.

The early Christians in both East and West set great store by the accounts of saints who helped the dead by their prayers.[10] One such account tells how St Perpetua, who died in AD 203, was imprisoned when her dead brother Denocrates appeared to her in a vision. He seemed to be wounded and unable to drink from a fountain, by which St Perpetua understood that he needed her prayers. She prayed daily for him to be taken into heaven and she was rewarded with another vision of him happy, healed, and able to drink from the eternal fountain.

This tradition of the saints helping the dead continues today in the Roman Catholic Church which particularly dedicates the month of November to them. On 2 November, it celebrates All Souls' Day by offering the Eucharist and prayers for them. Saints such as Teresa of Avila, Catherine of Bologna, and the Curé d'Ars were revered for their devotion in praying for the souls in purgatory (that is, the state of being purified) and the Council of Vienna in 1858 confirmed their belief that those in purgatory can intercede for the living. The Curé d'Ars explained, 'We must pray much for them so they may pray much for us.'

The Church of England also celebrates All Souls' Day. As one Anglican minister put it simply, 'For centuries people have celebrated funerals, usually some days after the person has died. If we can pray for a person three days after their death, surely we can continue to pray for them?' An Irish Baptist minister of my acquaintance objected strongly to this theory. Eventually, however, he shared with us the fact that at birth he was a twin, the other baby being a macerated male fetus which had been unceremoniously thrown away. 'Perhaps I killed him,' he said. 'We must pray for him tonight.'

An Anglican vicar wrote to me, 'I felt great reservations about your ideas on praying for the dead but recently I have discerned many passages, particularly in Hebrews, Ephesians and John which tell us that there are many areas in the heavens. In my Father's house are many rooms (John 14.2). It seems that there is one area in which many people seem to be working their passage towards the Lord, learning and receiving correction. These people are dependent on our ministry.' A few weeks later I received a postcard from him with the quotation from John 5.25: '. . . the dead will hear the voice of the Son of God . . .' This vicar has since celebrated the Eucharist of the Resurrection both within his own family and for others and has proved that, as a result, much healing has taken place.

Dr Raymond Moody's book *Life After Life*,[11,12] describing the experiences of resuscitated patients, supports the view that there seems to be a period of adjustment after death, for learning and receiving correction. Some of these patients report seeing a 'realm of bewildered spirits' in which the dead are trapped and trying to communicate with their living relatives in the hope of moving on to heaven. Since there is no time in eternity, this may be the stage when the prayers of the living are used by Jesus Christ to teach a dead person how to love and receive love.

It is surely an academic point whether or not prayer can be of any benefit to those who have committed great sins such as suicide. Even if they are condemned to hell and cannot comprehend love, it is surely right that the living should try to bring Jesus Christ to them in prayer because his presence binds all evil. The Eastern Orthodox Church[13] believes that praying for those in 'hell' gives them another chance to choose to be saved by Jesus Christ's mercy.

After listening to innumerable patients who have been near to suicide, many psychiatrists have deduced that the pressures these people face are so great that most of them are driven to commit the final act rather than freely choosing to do it. A close analogy is a man forced out of a burning building who hangs desperately on to a ledge until weakness and the force of gravity pull him to his death. Some patients think and talk about suicide only because they are being used by the possessing voice of an ancestor who went through the trauma of suicide and whose sin remains unexpiated. Thus they are not entirely to blame if, in fact, they commit the act and it may be argued that it is wrong for some churches to refuse to bury such people in consecrated ground or to give them a full service. We are not called upon to judge those who commit suicide and other evils but only to leave them in the Lord's mercy (Rom. 14.10). We consign many more people to hell than Jesus Christ would condemn.

An increasing number of Anglicans recognize that there exists – and that there is an absolute need for – an intermediate stage of 'purification' between death and resurrection. Probably, this stage is being described in 1 Peter 3.19–20, when Jesus Christ 'visited and preached to the spirits in prison who formerly did not obey'. That is, the sinner having died is no longer in the body but remains in the flesh. He is still very much earthbound and retains all of his desires and lusts; he is not free in the spiritual world. There, the unquiet spirits carry with them all the unresolved earthly battles of the flesh. They know no way out. Perhaps they are appealing to the living, but either we do not listen, or do not understand, or merely treat their urgent promptings as illnesses. We become aware of 'ghost hauntings' in some places, we recognize 'evil possession' in some people, we acknowledge the 'influence of ancestors' in some behaviour. In 1 Peter 4.6 the same idea is repeated but a stronger word is used in the original Greek – 'he went to evangelize the dead' – so therefore we can assume that a change was expected.

C. E. B. Cranfield, the biblical scholar, comments '. . . that interval (between death and resurrection) is not without significance, and in it, Jesus Christ is active as the Saviour of the world, and the scope of His saving activity is such that we dare set no limits to it'.[14] Since the unquiet souls are unable to free themselves, especially if they failed to choose, or even did not know, God's way when they were on earth, it is clear that someone must mediate for them. A group of Anglican theologians reporting to the Archbishop's Commission on Christian Doctrine[15] write of how the living may usefully pray for the dead, through

Jesus Christ, that during the state of purification they may develop 'a deepening of character and a greater maturity of personality'. When they are ready to give and receive total love and can grow into the image of Jesus Christ, they can then proceed to the everlasting 'beatific vision'.

I have been at hundreds of deathbeds in the past fifty years. Many have died in misery and with fear; but countless numbers have died with delight, clearly seeing something exciting and joyful in the adventure they were about to begin. One man of seventy-eight, who had been a deaf mute all his life, suddenly sat up in his bed, his usually unsmiling face alight with happiness, raised both arms and with his last breath shouted 'Father'. Three days before my own father died, he told us that a crowd of his friends had appeared to tell him that they would return to collect him at a certain hour. He was delighted by this vision and, indeed, he died on the stroke of the hour that had been foretold. Our 'loss' turned to rejoicing: we did not need to shed tears. We thanked God for my father's life here – his time as a surgeon, his thirty-seven years spent in the creation of China's medical and scientific literature – and we knew that he was active and happy, still doing God's work somewhere.

For those, who during their lifetime either did not know how to or did not want to follow the Lord and who no longer have free will, it seems that we, the living, have some responsibility, some authority according to our own state of grace, to plead forgiveness for their sins, their faults and their ignorance, so that now they may be shown the way to God.

It is not permitted, however, to make direct contact with them. We are expressly told that to do so is in absolute contravention of God's law. We may not pray *to* the dead;

we are required to pray *for* the dead. We must act, as it were, in the third person and refer them to the Lord for him to deal with. It is selfish and cruel to try to 'hang on to them' or to 'call them back'. They await release, not restriction to earthly things and people.

William Barclay in his book, *The Plain Man's Guide to the Apostle's Creed*, says this: 'The word for punishment (Matthew 25.46) is "kolasis". This word was originally a gardening word and its original meaning was "pruning trees" . . . It can therefore be seen that the phrase in Matthew . . . does not commit us to a doctrine of eternal punishment in the sense in which it is usually taken. It may well describe a disciplinary, curative punishment and it certainly describes the punishment which only God can inflict.'

Prayers

1. PREFACE

In the following pages I have attempted to set down the pictures and words which came to me in a vision. In my vision it was as clear as the words spoken so I prayed to be able to draw in outline the vision as I saw it. This is exactly as it came through the brushwork without any correction and the words are just as I heard them.

Jesus said 'in this manner pray ye'. It is important that we note this is no vain repetition. We waste our time in its speedy recitation . . . and some Christians even refuse to say this prayer.

The sequence of the Lord's Prayer follows man's own development and growing insight in his spiritual pilgrimage. In my vision he used his body as the diagram. The Holy Spirit made this all real to the disciples after Pentecost.

Whenever we say the Lord's Prayer we may recall that he is saying this with us. He is present and we should be looking at him. He is visible and is joining us in talking to the Father.

OUR FATHER IN HEAVEN

HALLOWED BE THY NAME

THY KINGDOM COME

THY WILL BE DONE

ON EARTH AS IN HEAVEN ABOVE

GIVE US THIS DAY OUR DAILY BREAD

FORGIVE US OUR TRESPASSES

AS WE FORGIVE THOSE

WHO TRESPASS AGAINST US

BE WITH US IN TEMPTATION

AND DELIVER US

FROM THE EVIL ONE

OUR FATHER IN HEAVEN

HALLOWED

BE THY NAME

Our Father in heaven, hallowed be thy name

Imagine Jesus' arms above his head.

'OUR Father'
  Not MY but OUR – on a level with us.
  What humility!

FATHER, ABBA, 'DADDY' –
  No longer the idea of a remote thunderbolt-throwing
  deity.

Our relationship – the highest point of our contact,
  above the heads of most of us.

The upraised arms in an attitude of surrender.

The upraised arms point to the heaven we long to
  experience and which we begin to experience now in
  his presence.

We will respect his name and his designation.

THY KINGDOM

COME

THIS IS WHAT YOU'RE TO DO

Thy kingdom come

We want your kingdom to come.

It is the product of our hands.

We represent you here on earth.

As we do so we begin to become part now of your eternal kingdom in our hearts.

Jesus' right hand is outstretched and he brought the palm forward.

THY WILL BE DONE
THIS IS THE GUIDANCE
YOU ARE TO RECEIVE

Thy will be done

Your guidance is what we need.

We will spend time in silence, listening and looking.

We receive with one hand upturned and will write it
  down with the other hand.

We were designed in your own image –
  your creative purpose,
  a person you long to communicate with.

ON EARTH

ON YOUR SHOULDERS

AS IN

HEAVEN ABOVE

120

On earth as in heaven above

With his left hand on his own shoulder he says 'ON EARTH'.

We carry it on our own shoulders.

The responsibility of seeing his will done falls on us. We have free will here to choose the path we take – to help others to choose, to set forth your way to others.

With his right hand pointed upwards, he says, 'as it is in heaven'.

And we model this on our concept of heaven – joy, peace, light, warmth
    and, above all, love.

Our relationship to God is now in order, so we turn to our own selves and our needs.

GIVE US THIS DAY
OUR DAILY BREAD
AND ALL WE NEED

Give us this day our daily bread and all we need

With his right hand he takes, as it were, food and
   clothing.

Our daily bread and all we need for our bodies . . .
   food
      clothes
         shelter.

'The birds of the air they neither sow nor reap nor
   gather into barns . . . the flowers of the field, they
   neither toil nor spin . . .'

His provision is there for all our own needs, for health
   and healing too.

'There is enough for everyone's need but not for
   everyone's greed.'

Waste not – want less.

FORGIVE US OUR

TRESPASSES

Forgive us our trespasses

Then he lays his left hand on his heart.

We receive with our left hand
   and take it to heart.

Forgiveness – no longer to be earned but accepted – a
   gift from God, through his last and final sacrifice, the
   shedding of the innocent blood of his beloved Son.

Therefore no more sacrifices of blood were ever to be
   performed again.

AS WE FORGIVE

THOSE WHO TRESPASS

AGAINST US

INCLUDING OUR ANCESTORS

As *we forgive those who trespass against us*

With his right hand clenched he brings it like a punch
    into his solar plexus.

Here is a new factor, totally unexpected.

The idea that we should forgive others, even our
    enemies, those who would hurt or destroy us.

This is what you, Lord Jesus, did.

You even underwent the dreaded death and conquered
    it, making death now no more to be feared but
    welcomed.

And opened the gates of heaven to those too that were
    dead.

Only as we forgive can we be forgiven.

BE WITH US

IN TEMPTATION

Be with us in temptation

He places both hands on his hips.

He is with us when we are tempted ...
   over money
      over sex
         or the way we walk in life.

He does not tempt us –
   he is exactly the opposite.

So we are saying 'remind us of your presence when we
   are tempted and give us the strength to turn from it'.

There was a pause.

The second phase is completed.

We have been personally dealt with, and all is in order.

Our relationship is right with God and our neighbours.

Now we are ready at last to pray the prayer to be
   delivered from evil.

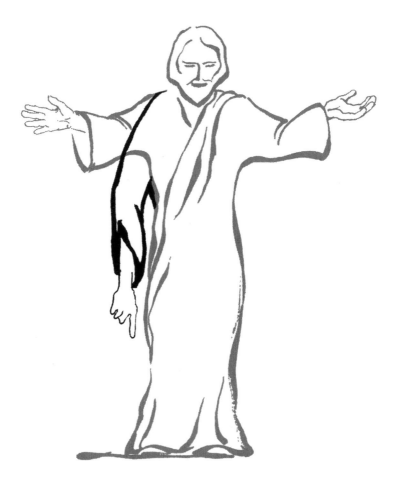

AND DELIVER US

FROM THE EVIL ONE

TRODDEN UNDER FOOT –
that's all the attention Satan gets

And deliver us from the evil one

Jesus' finger points firmly down –
   He says 'Yes, deliver us.'

We have no power.
   It is his to deliver us from evil, not only in ourselves
   but also from the evil one himself.
   'If I by the finger of God cast out Satan.'

Here is Paul's battle, not against flesh and blood, but
   against principalities and powers, the spiritual hosts
   of wickedness.

We are alive.

We have free will.

We can live in bondage.

Or we can choose to live in the power of the Holy Spirit
   in light, love and freedom.

Satan cannot stand in Jesus' presence.

Then we say
    AMEN ...
    so be it

No longer do I see our Lord standing in front of me but he comes and kneels or sits beside me in a brown working gown, saying this prayer with me to the Father.

Then we can discuss problems together and he tells me what to do.

2. THE EUCHARIST OF THE RESURRECTION

At the Eucharist we should always have specific intentions. Perhaps 1 per cent for ourselves, 99 per cent for others.

Our prayers should be spoken aloud, shared with others we trust – especially family members. Best in a private Eucharist and prayed before the confession. If this is to be included in a public service, then sit outside in the car beforehand. If in a service especially established for this purpose for many families, then they can come up to the altar during the offertory and lay their Family Trees and requests there and say aloud their prayers with several families talking at once. Be specific in naming the sins.

To say them aloud makes the whole objective and takes the symptoms outside the patient, who can now hear and consciously cathect the situation.

Let us pray.

God our Father in heaven, we bow in your presence and thank you for sparing your only Son.

We know that you, our Lord Jesus Christ, are risen from the dead. You are alive and here with us. Please now direct your angels to gather all our deceased that seem to be lost, especially _____ and many others whom you know but whom we have omitted. Bring them where you wish that they may see your broken body, healed and risen so that in their brokenness they too might rise. Let them receive your blood poured out, a completed act for the forgiveness of their sins.

Blind and banish Satan and his minions to their appropriate place.

Let the Body and Blood of our Lord heal all the wounds and torments inflicted by Satan and his minions on the living and the dead.

Father, we come as stumbling children who neither understand nor know how to pray. Send your Holy Spirit to intercede for us.

We ask this in the name of our Lord Jesus Christ – Amen.

3. THE COMMUNION SERVICE

The Lord's Prayer

The Rite of Forgiveness

We and our departed ones have sinned before you
All: Lord, have mercy

We and our departed ones have failed to forgive one another
All: Lord, have mercy

We and our departed ones have failed to forgive our ancestors.
All: Lord, have mercy

Collect Prayer (one or more of the following may be used)

Almighty, everlasting God, who has dominion both of the living and the dead: we humbly beseech you for your servant(s) _____ , that he (she) may obtain of your bountiful goodness the remission of all his (her) sins: through your Son Jesus Christ our Lord, who with you in the unity of the Holy Spirit, lives and reigns, God, world without end. Amen.

O Lord, grant rest to the soul of your servant _____ , that he (she) may repose in a place where there is no pain, no grief, no sighing, but everlasting life. Amen.

O Lord, grant to this your servant to rest with the righteous ones and to dwell in your courts, as it is written. Since you are merciful God, forgive his (her) sins, and all his (her) transgressions that he (she) has committed by thought, word, or deed, knowingly or unknowingly, for you are the lover of mankind, now and always and for ever and ever. Amen.

O Saviour, you are God. You descended into Hades to deliver those who were bound there in suffering; grant rest also to the soul(s) of this (these) your departed servant(s). Glory to the Father and to the Son and to the Holy Spirit; now and always and for ever and ever. Amen.

Readings (choose one or another)

Isa. 25.6–9 – wipe away every tear
2 Macc. 12.38–45 – it is good to pray for the dead

Rom. 6.3–9 – if we die with Christ, we will live with him
1 Cor. 15.51–57 – death is swallowed up in victory
1 John 3.1–2 – we shall be like God

Matt. 27.51–54 – the saints freed

Luke 8.49–56 – Jairus	Luke 18.15–17 – Jesus and babies
John 6.35–40 – raise him up	John 6.51–58 – Bread of life
John 14.1–6 – many mansions	John 11.39–44 – Lazarus

Prayer at Offering the Bread and Wine

(After the gospel, the bread and wine are placed on the altar together with the names of those who are to be remembered.)

Prayer of Consecration

Communion

I am the resurrection and the life; he who believes in me, though he die yet shall he live, and whoever lives and believes in me shall never die.

Prayer after Communion (*choose one or another*)

We give you thanks our God and King, for the joy of this heavenly banquet, and we beseech you that the sacrament of your Body and Blood may not turn to our condemnation, but be for us and all the departed, especially _____, the cleansing of sin, the strengthening of weakness, and our strong defence against all adversity; through your mercy, O Saviour of the world, who lives and reigns with the Father in the unity of the Holy Spirit, one God world without end. Amen.

Expectantly awaiting our own resurrection, we celebrate also the future transfiguration of the whole created order in harmony and beauty. Lord you have made the world for joy and you lead souls from the depth of sin to holiness. Grant to the dead a new life in the unchanging light of the Lamb of God, and may we celebrate with them the eternal Passover. Amen. (From Prayers by a Russian Bishop)

Remember your servant, O Lord, according to the favour that you bear unto your people, and grant that increasing in knowledge and love of you, he (she) may go from strength to strength and attain to the fulness of joy in your heavenly kingdom: through Jesus Christ our Lord, who lives and reigns with you, and the Holy Spirit now and forever. Amen. (From Liturgy of Episcopal Church of Scotland).

Blessing

May God the Father Almighty continue to heal you that you may have more of his love for the living and the dead. We ask this blessing in the name of the Father, and of the Son, and of the Holy Spirit.
All: Amen.

4. BLESSING OF A HOME

Our help is in the name of the Lord
All: Who made heaven and earth
The Lord be with you
All: May He also be with you

Let us pray.

God the Father Almighty, we fervently implore for the sake of this home and its occupants and possessions, that You may bless _____ and sanctify them, enriching them by your kindness in every way possible. Pour out on them, Lord, heavenly dew in good measure, as well as an abundance of earthly needs. Mercifully listen to their prayers, and grant that their desires be fulfilled. At our lowly coming be pleased to bless _____ and sanctify this home, as you once were pleased to bless the home of Abraham, Isaac and Jacob. Within these walls let your angels of light preside and stand watch over those who live here; through Christ our Lord.

All: Amen.

The doorstep is sprinkled with holy water.

(Blessing from *The Roman Ritual* by Philip Weller, Milwaukee: Bruce Publishing Company, 1964, or *Exorcism* by Dom Robert Petitpierre, London: SPCK, 1972).

Notes

Chapter 2

1. P. M. Yap, 'The Possession Syndrome', *Journal of Mental Science*, 106, 1960.
2. For further information on the issues discussed in this chapter, see Carl Jung, 'Possession is caused by something that could perhaps most fitly be described as an "ancestral soul".' *The Archetypes and the Collective Unconscious*, 124; R. K. McAll, 'Demonosis or the Possession Syndrome', *International Journal of Social Psychiatry*, 17.2, Spring 1971.

Chapter 3

1. St Elizabeth's daughter, Constance, was freed after 365 masses. Constance had appeared and said she was languishing but could be released if the Eucharist was celebrated for her every day for a year. Later Constance reappeared in a brilliant white robe. 'Today,' she told her mother Elizabeth, 'I am delivered from the pains of purgatory.' Elizabeth went to tell the good news to the priest Mendez. Mendez assured her that on the previous day he had finished offering the 365th mass for Queen Constance. It also took St Thomas Aquinas many masses before he saw his deceased sister freed from suffering and going to heaven. However, knowing her brother's inquisitive mind, his sister stopped to tell St Thomas Aquinas several things. She told him that his brother Landolph was in purgatory, that his brother Emperor Frederic was in heaven, and that a magnificent place awaited him in heaven. St Thomas died shortly after receiving the news from his sister that a place was waiting him in heaven. While

St Elizabeth and St Thomas found it necessary to offer more than one mass, St Teresa of Avila knew that their benefactor, Medina del Campo, would be released to heaven as soon as they could offer a mass in the new convent they were building. At the first mass while going to communion, St Teresa saw Medina del Campo 'with hands joined and countenance all radiant, thanking me for having delivered him from purgatory'. (P. W. Keppler, *Pour Souls in Purgatory* (St Louis: Herder, 1927), 158, 271, 179.)

Chapter 5

1. The correlation of maternal stress during pregnancy with birth defects is researched by D. H. Stott and Sandra Latchford, 'Prenatal Antecedents of Child Health, Development and Behavior', *J. Am. Academy of Child Psychiatry*, 15, 161–91, 1976.
2. David Spelt ten years previously had already shown that the human fetus in the last two months can be conditioned to respond to a loud noise. David Spelt, 'Conditioning of the Human Fetus in Utero', *J. Experimental Psychology*, 38, 338–46, 1948.
3. Reported in *Chicago Tribune*, 'Embryos Can Remember, Therapist Says', 1 Nov. 1978.
4. Conrad Baars, MD, *Feeling and Healing Your Emotions*, (Plainfield: Logos, 1979), 82–4.
5. Joan Fitzherbert, 'The Source of Man's Intimations of Immortality', *British Journal of Psychiatry*, 110, 1964.

Chapter 6

1. Kurt Koch, *Christian Counseling and Occultism* (Grand Rapids: Kregel, 1972), 189.

Chapter 7

1. Transcendental meditation (TM) is dangerous for the Christian since it involves initiation through a Hindu puja

ceremony and mantras often invoking deities. The supreme court upheld the court of New Jersey declaring the Hindu religious nature of TM that could not be supported by public funds.

2. For how to pray for inner healing cf. Ruth Stapleton, *The Gift of Inner Healing* (Waco, TX: Word, 1976); Dennis and Matthew Linn, *Healing Life's Hurts* (New York: Paulist, 1978).

3. Pat Brooks, *Using Your Spiritual Authority* (Monroeville, PA: Banner, 1973), 85.

4. Kurt Koch, *Occult Bondage and Deliverance* (Grand Rapids: Kregel, 1970), 100.

5. Kurt Koch, *Christian Counseling and Occultism* (Grand Rapids: Kregel, 1972), 307.

6. For an excellent, concise treatment on praying for deliverance cf. Francis MacNutt, *Healing* (Notre Dame: Ave Maria, 1974), 208–31. A fuller presentation is John Richards, *But Deliver Us From Evil* (London: Darton, Longman and Todd, 1974).

7. For how to pray for inner healing of the hurt and traumas see Theodore Dobson, *Inner Healing: God's Great Assurance* (New York: Paulist, 1978); Linn, Matthew and Dennis, *Healing of Memories* (New York: Paulist, 1974), *Healing Life's Hurts* (New York: Paulist, 1978); Agnes Sanford, *The Healing Gifts of the Spirit* (Worcestershire: Arthur James Ltd, 1966); Ruth Stapleton, *Gift of Inner Healing* (New York: Bantam, 1977), *The Experience of Inner Healing* (Waco, TX: Word, 1977); Betty Tapscott, *Inner Healing Through Healing of Memories* (Houston: Box 19827, 1975).

8. Dr. Kurt Koch through dealing with hundreds of occult cases also highly recommends the Eucharist as the key to staying free. 'In the Lord's Supper the person liberated from occult subjection is brought into participation in the Christ event. The liberated person experiences by means of visible signs his fellowship with the body and blood of Christ, his

incorporation into the Church of Christ, the realization of membership in the Kingdom, and thus the strengthening of his spiritual resistance against demonic influences and attacks ... Therefore I recommend a frequent attendance at the Lord's Supper for the person who has been liberated from occult subjection. As a marginal note I would suggest that the churches should make the sacrament more available than it has been up to now.' (Koch, *Christian Counseling*, 332).

Chapter 8

1. The early fathers interpreted 1 Cor. 3.11–15 as referring to an intermediate state of purification. Robert Bellarmine, *De Purg.* I,5 cites passages from Sts Ambrose, Augustine, Jerome, Gregory and Origen.

2. Joseph Wilpert, *Die Malereien der Katakomben Roms*, 334, quoted in P. W. Keppler, *Poor Souls in Purgatory* (St Louis: Herder, 1927), 27.

3. John Chrysostom, *1 Ad Cor.*, Hom. XLI, n. 4, P. G., LXI, col. 361, 362. Cyprian, Ep. 1, 2 CSEL III, 466f.

4. Joseph Jungmann, *Mass of the Roman Rite* (New York: Benziger Bros. 1959), 441–3.

5. Tertullian, *De Monog*, 10:4; *Corp Christ* 2:1043 and 2:1243.

6. Eusebius, *Life of Constantine* 4:71; GCS 7:147.

7. Jungmann, *Mass of the Roman Rite*, 443.

8. *Apostolic Constitution*, P. G. I, Col. 1144.

9. John Chrysostom, Hom 3 in *Ep ad Phil.*, n. 4.

10. Alban Butler, *Lives of the Saints* (New York: Kennedy, 1956) I, 495.

11. Raymond Moody, *Life After Life* (Covington: Mockingbird, 1975).

12. Raymond Moody, *Reflections on Life After Life* (New York: Bantam, 1977), 18–22.

13. Sergei Bulgakov, *The Orthodox Church* (London: Centenary, 1935), 208–9.

14. C. E. B. Cranfield, *The First Epistle of Peter* (London: SCM).

15. *Prayer and the Departed*, Archbishops' Commission on Christian Doctrine (London: SPCK, 1971, 20). Few people would feel that at death they were sufficiently mature for the direct vision of God or for his immediate presence; nor would they presume that engrained habits of sin could be immediately eradicated. To hold that any Christian, even the most faithful, will be transformed into immediate perfection at death seems to many people incredible and verging on magic. It would seem that the turning of a sinful person – even of a person who desired the consummation of the vision of God – into the divine likeness cannot be an instantaneous process if human nature and free will and the continuity of the individual personality across the divide of death are to be respected. In any case, since felicity as known in this life is temporal, and a temporal situation (at least as we know it here) is a context for action and development, how is it possible to picture a state after death in which such temporal characteristics as joy and felicity, though they are posited of persons, yet have no development? All these considerations make many Christians incline to the belief that development is possible after death; if this is so, then prayers of intercession are in order. We could be forbidden to intercede only if the situation towards which our prayers were directed was unalterably static. Prayers for the development of the departed need not imply any doubt on our part as to the outcome of their further pilgrimage, as though they could be assured of salvation at the time of death and yet lose their way thereafter. They may rather be prayers for deepening of character and for a greater maturity of personality. Nor need prayers for light and peace imply a present lack. We may always pray for an increase (or even a continuance) of what is currently being enjoyed by the people for whom we pray.

Author's Postscript

In the past six months a number of people have followed the ideas and suggestions in this book by themselves without reference to their doctor or priest. They have attended a regular Eucharist with the intent of committing their Family Tree to God and asking forgiveness for past wrongs. As a result there have been healings, not only in themselves, but in distant relatives as well.

A woman who had suffered with migraine ever since she was a child was healed in this way. This was in spite of the fact that she knew nothing about her Family Tree. Her old father had become confused and could remember nothing about his ancestry. After the service, not only was she healed but, on visiting her father, she found him with a completely clear mind and restored memory.

A couple who had been separated, came together again after one of them had attended such a service.

One group of people went together to the Eucharist to pray for and commit members of the family who had died violently at the hands of other members. During the service they had visions of those who had been released in the next world. Later they discovered that the culprits who had caused the disaster, and were in prison or mental hospitals as a result, had been converted the morning of the service.

There is a great deal to be gained by members of the family concerned praying aloud so that they consciously hear their own words. It also helps to confirm their intention when prayers are said aloud in the presence of others. This can more easily be done at a private Eucharist and can then be followed up by the silent personal prayers said at subsequent Eucharists.

Much theological discussion has been engendered by this book especially among clergy and their bishops. I have learned from them that our authority to do these things comes from the teaching of the Lord Jesus Christ and that his instructions are as true now for us as they were then.

In the stories of his work it is clear that he expected those concerned to take some part in the healing process. When he said, 'Let the little children come to me,' he expected their mothers to bring them. At the tomb of Lazarus our Lord instructed those present – the disciples and the family, to roll away the stone. After he had called Lazarus out of the tomb, the family were given the task of unbinding him.

At the raising of Jairus' daughter, our Lord specifically told three of his disciples and the girl's parents to *go* with him into the room. After he had brought her back to life, he instructed the parents to give her something to eat. They were involved at every stage.

The centurion's act of faith and love in coming himself to Jesus was a necessary part of his servant's healing. The blind beggar had to put into words himself exactly what it was he wanted of Jesus.

One of my own recent cases was put in touch with me by the nurse who was looking after him. He was an elderly man who had lost his right arm in the First World War and had suffered intolerable phantom pain ever since, becoming addicted first to morphine and later to physeptone. The shell which had wounded him had blown to pieces four of his closest friends. They had never had a funeral because as he said, 'There was nothing left to bury.'

Being a priest himself, he readily agreed to arrange for a Eucharist at which his friends were committed to God. From that day to his death a few months later, he had no more severe pain and no further need of drugs.

Another area in which this approach has made an impact is Northern Ireland. There the men of violence, some of whom I met, claim that the authority for doing what they do, comes from those who have died. They carry on in their name. To me it looks like skeletons of the past fighting other skeletons of the past. They are yesterday's people fighting yesterday's battles, the battles of three hundred years ago. Both sides in the struggle bury their dead in anger and with vows of revenge. The traditional words concerning the 'faithful departed' seem quite inappropriate. There is no apology to God and those lost souls continue to haunt and influence their descendants. Satan will take advantage of every occult force to divide, destroy and control. People need to realize that they act as Satan's puppets and are lost themselves. A book by Robert Cielou – *Spare My Tortured People* – enlarges on this idea.

The same pattern can be seen in all the fighting and violence around the world where people appear to be pawns in a vast battle of occult forces.

Therefore in our mourning and in confession we need to do our best to be specific in our prayers. Healing occurs where this happens. In seven separate diabetic families the original sufferer in each family was the one who had carried the equivalent to 'a punch in the stomach' from other family members – in one case for five generations. Now all the families have been healed.

A seventy-eight-year-old lady, a polio victim, went to a Eucharist to praise God for all he had done for her family, and she laid the Family Tree on the altar. To everyone's surprise and delight she awoke the next morning with a normal leg. She had been paralysed and numb in her left side with polio since the age of sixteen.

We who stand at a safe distance, or who think we are safe, are equally responsible. We should all go to our own Eucharist services in sorrow and contrition. Over one hundred and thirty anorexia nervosa patients have been helped by this service. It is being suggested that Holy Innocents Day, 28 December, should become a day of national mourning for all the year's abortions.

Index

29531221R00093

Printed in Great Britain
by Amazon